JANE

A Pin Up at War

JANE
A Pin Up at War

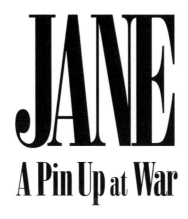

Andy Saunders

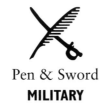

Pen & Sword
MILITARY

First published in Great Britain in 2004 by Leo Cooper.

Published in this format in 2005 by
Pen & Sword Military
An imprint of
Pen & Sword Books Ltd
47 Church Street
Barnsley
South Yorkshire
S70 2AS

ISBN 1 84415 292 8

A CIP catalogue record for this book is
available from the British Library

Printed and bound in England
By CPI UK

Pen & Sword Books Ltd incorporates the Imprints of Pen & Sword Aviation,
Pen & Sword Maritime, Pen & Sword Military, Wharncliffe Local history, Pen & Sword Select,
Pen & Sword Military Classics and Leo Cooper.

For a complete list of Pen & Sword titles please contact
PEN & SWORD BOOKS LIMITED
47 Church Street, Barnsley, South Yorkshire, S70 2AS, England
E-mail: enquiries@pen-and-sword.co.uk
Website: www.pen-and-sword.co.uk

Contents

INTRODUCTION vii

ACKNOWLEDGEMENTS ix

CHAPTER ONE   A BRIGHT YOUNG THING 1

CHAPTER TWO   THE EARLY YEARS: BLITZY AND
                     FRITZI...16

CHAPTER THREE   MARRY ME, JANE! 29

CHAPTER FOUR   JANE ON STAGE..38

CHAPTER FIVE   OF NUDES AND PRUDES...............................64

CHAPTER SIX   OF TANKS, BOATS AND PLANES 81

CHAPTER SEVEN   I REMEMBER JANE!......................................100

CHAPTER EIGHT   JANE – USA STYLE 118

CHAPTER NINE   INTO THE SUNSET...126

CHAPTER TEN   JUST JANE – ALWAYS JANE.........................141

William Norman Pett, Creator of Jane, 1891–1960................................163

Introduction

"Without Jane", said Wing Commander H.R. "Dizzy" Allen DFC, "the war would have been a very dull affair indeed." As a decorated RAF fighter ace, Allen's war must have been anything *but* dull. That said, there was a common perception that the war was 99% boredom and just 1% excitement, so Allen was probably speaking for the majority of servicemen when expressing his sentiments about Jane, the wartime pin-up. She certainly helped fill some of the 99% whilst becoming an iconic figure of World War Two. Her story will forever remain a significant piece of British social and military history.

The delightful creation of gifted artist Norman Pett, Jane was a daily strip cartoon in the *Daily Mirror* that captured the imagination of millions during the dark days of World War Two. Drawn from, amongst others, the life model of Chrystabel Leighton-Porter, the artwork of Pett was transformed into treasured pin-ups for British troops and lifted morale with her unlikely adventures. Inevitably, those adventures ended with Jane's clothes being torn off her, lost, or interestingly re-arranged in some way. Total nudity, however, did not occur until just after D-Day and can be considered a milestone in the history of newspaper publishing and, indeed, the story of the pin-up in Britain's social history. That said, there remained a certain naïveté and innocence about Jane that did not cross the threshold of what might be described as the rather more vulgar page three pin-up models of later years. After all, these were just innocent drawings – not photographs leaving nought to the imagination!

That Jane was drawn from more than one model during her existence did not matter. Jane was still Jane whoever she was. However, that Chrystabel Leighton-Porter *became* Jane was due largely to the fact that she presented the Jane stage shows and, through that, almost grew into the living persona of the character. She lived the part, and loved it. Jane's fans loved her for it, too. This then is the story of Jane, cartoon character and wartime pin-up – *and* Britain's secret weapon!

Andy Saunders, Hastings, Sussex, 2003.

Acknowledgements

A great many people have assisted to a greater or lesser degree in the production of this book. My thanks go to them all, but in particular I must mention those who have made significant contributions, especially the late Chrystabel Leighton-Porter, her husband Arthur, and their son Simon. Of special note, however, is my old pal Cliff White and his wife Jill. They were long time family friends of Chrystabel, Arthur and Simon and were enthusiastic Jane fans who have long appreciated the importance of Jane's role in wartime Britain. Without Cliff's input this book would have been much the poorer and so much more difficult to write. Time and again he came up with gems of information, together with countless leads and contacts. Thank you Cliff. I must also thank Gina Sheridan, Norman Pett's grand-daughter, for her invaluable assistance. In addition, Winston Ramsey, John Frost, Terry Parker, Chris Butler, Roger Freeman and Squadron Leader Chris Goss. Dr Christopher Dowling at the Imperial War Museum has also provided long-term assistance and support. Additional photographic work was expertly and enthusiastically carried out by Jane Keen and Andy Clark. Last, but by no means least, must I mention Zoë, whom I thank for enthusing, cajoling, encouraging and for persuading me to stop procrastinating and complete this long-talked-about project! Without her it would not have happened. I can only hope that Chrystabel, or Jane for that matter, would have liked this book and derived even half as much fun from reading it as I had in researching and writing it.

For my eldest daughter, Clare

Comic Strip

I do not like the comic strip,
   (Except the one of Jane!),
Old Popeye's pranks give me the pip,
Just Jake gives me a pain.

'Lil Moner and his Daisy Mae,
The trials of Bucky Ryan,
Like every dog, have had their day,
And that there's no denyin'.

So take away the comic....wait!
What's this? The *Union Jack!*
Excuse me, please, I have a date,
With Jane upon the back!

*By Gunner J. Milne, Royal Artillery, while based in Eboli, Italy,
February 1945.*

Chapter One

A Bright Young Thing

Sitting in his opulent London office at the Fetter Lane headquarters of the *Daily Mirror* during the summer of 1932, the News Group Chairman Harry Bartholomew flicked through the archived children's strip cartoons of Pip, Squeak & Wilfred. Just how, he wondered, might it be possible to create strips that had the same mass appeal to adults? Determined to find a way, he turned to the exceptional cartoon artist Norman Pett and instructed him to come up with an idea, "... something memorable", growled Bartholomew. To Pett, the choice of words struck a chord and the result was "Jane's Journal – The Diary of a Bright Young Thing". The rest, as they say, is history – but suffice it to say that the Mass Observation Organisation was moved to later state in their 1949 survey of the Press that: "Much of the popularity of the *Mirror* strips may be due to their blending of reality and fantasy in such a way that people are easily stimulated into identifying themselves with the strip characters". Bartholomew had achieved his aim, and Pett had given his newspaper a ground-breaking winner with this blending of "reality and fantasy". As will be seen, an unexpected element of reality was later to be given to Pett's Jane in the comely shape of one of his life models.

First, though, let us ask the question: who *was* Jane, the cartoon character?

Aside from the obvious, *Picture Post* succinctly set out its own biographical sketch of who they believed Jane was, telling its readers:

> "Jane is not a girl of strong feelings, nor is she any mental giant. She is just a long-legged presentable-looking blonde of great courage and generosity. Her standards are upper middle class, but not too upper. Financially she is not very well off, though she has comfortable colonial parents somewhere in the dim background. She likes the company of Officers. She has a regular young man of her own, a patient, simple and rather dull character named Georgie. But she does not seem wildly interested in him. Georgie was an Intelligence Officer, though not a terribly intelligent one.
>
> "To the psychologists she promotes widespread erotic infantilism. To her admirers she is a big-hearted inviolable heroine, immeasurably generous, striding through a blood-and-thunder world, shedding her clothes on all sides, with no other intention than to please." That, then, was Norman Pett's Jane.

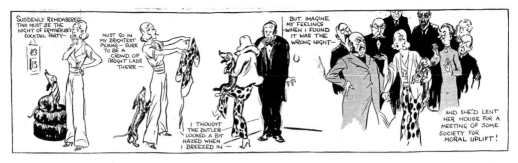

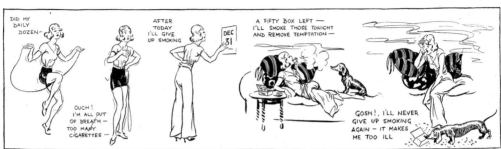

The original Daily Mirror *Jane* cartoon was called "The Diary of a Bright Young Thing" and ran from December 1932. Drawn by Norman Pett, and employing his wife Mary as the model, the strip had none of its later raciness. When it later became just simply *Jane*, the format, style and storylines changed – to include the parting of Jane from her clothes as a regular feature. This is some early Pett artwork for the Daily Mirror *Bright Young Thing* cartoon strip and includes comments by the newspaper's cartoon editor back to the artist.

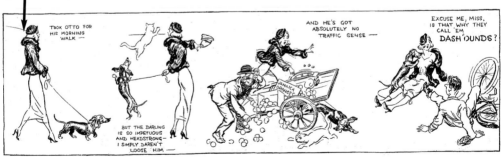

Pett was born in 1891 in Birmingham, the son of a city jeweller, and went on to study at the Press Art School where he honed his talent under the guidance of Percy Bradshaw who was to predict that Pett would, in time, create "... something memorable". It was to be an uncannily accurate prediction, echoed years later in Bartholomews's gruff instructions. Fate, though, may well have taken a different path. Service as an infantryman during the First World War had almost cut short this promising talent when Pett fell victim to a gas attack, the effects of which were to plague him for the rest of his days and caused his medical discharge. Military service did, however, give him an insight into the soldier's psyche and how the army worked – as it happened, valuable experience that would come into its own for Pett during the Second World War.

It was on 5 December 1932, though, that Pett's memorable creation first came to life, originally as a daily strip of four to five drawings each and featuring a tall, shapely and somewhat dizzy blonde. At first, it was to be on the basis of a one-month trial. Each strip was, in itself, a complete short story and featured Jane, the Bright Young Thing, in a whole range of jolly escapades with her little Dachshund dog, Otto. Initially, for these early strips, Pett was both artist and storyline writer. During this period, and although every opportunity was seized by Pett to show off Jane's lithe figure, there was no hint, yet, of any state of nudity or partial undress. The world of 1932, it seemed, was not yet ready for the racier Jane of later years. Indeed, one of the strips makes an interesting social comment on the acceptability, or otherwise, of certain female dress of the nineteen thirties. In it, a scatterbrained Jane turns up for a cocktail party held, perhaps inevitably, by the Society for Moral Uplift and dressed, shock horror, in only her pyjamas! By this time, of course, Pett's probationary period had passed and been endorsed with an open-ended agreement. But things would change with the strip, and perhaps it is true to say that this change began to set in when Pett's wife, Mary, withdrew her services as the life model for a hapless Jane. Officially, this has been attributed to the fact that Mary had developed a passion for golf and was unwilling to devote time for sittings when she could be out on the greens. In reality it was more likely that the lovely Mary had passed her first flush of youth and Pett knew he needed another model. Already, though, Bartholomew's foresight had brought measurable and profitable results from what was seemingly a mediocre strip cartoon. What was around the corner was nothing short of unbelievably sensational, and would have a colossal effect on *Daily Mirror* sales, revolutionise certain aspects of newspaper publishing and impact upon the nation as a whole. The phenomenon of Jane was about to unfold. In the fullest sense of the word, it would be truly unique.

"That's Jane!" exclaimed Pett when he set eyes upon life-model Chrystabel Leighton-Porter posing for an art class at the Birmingham

Central School of Art. The year, it seems, must have been 1938. According to Chrystabel, her twin sister was an artist, and it was she who had encouraged her to pose for life art classes. Chrystabel, a petite blue-eyed blonde, appeared to Norman the very epitome of what the "new" Jane ought to be as soon as he set eyes on her and he immediately set about re-inventing what had become a flagging cartoon. Initially, however, Chrystabel was understandably wary of this middle-aged man who wanted to take her home and draw her in the nude! To put her at ease, Pett's wife Mary collected her in her car for her first drawing assignment and Chrystabel immediately struck up a friendship with both artist and wife. It was a friendship which endured until Pett's death, and was the start of a remarkable partnership and journey. It was also a journey upon which Chrystabel enthusiastically embarked, and a partnership that would see mutual and lasting benefits for both artist and model alike. In time, Chrystabel would "become" Jane in more than name alone and, indeed, to her husband and all who knew her she was called Jane more often than Chrystabel. However, only now has it become possible to tell the full story behind the artist, Jane the cartoon girl and Jane the character as personified by Chrystabel Leighton-Porter.

Born into what her family would subsequently describe as almost grinding poverty on 11 April 1913, Chrystabel Drury was one of twin sisters in a family of eleven children of whom only eight survived beyond childhood. She was the daughter of an Eastleigh railway worker, and for Chrystabel and her twin sister Sylvia, life would probably only promise domestic service or, at best, some equally menial job as a shop assistant, but from an early age Chrystabel carried a single-minded and burning determination to better herself. Possessed of a wonderful figure, the teenage Chrystabel developed a passion for tennis and swimming and in particular, became an accomplished swimmer with the Kingston 43 Swimming Club. Doubtless her sporting prowess served to hone an already perfect physique, such that it would lead to her part-time work as a life model for artists, and as a photographer's model in various art studios. It was also here, in Birmingham, that Pett's chance encounter would follow upon the submission by photographer Bertram Park of his tasteful photographic studies of the young Chrystabel to "Britain's Perfect Girl" competition. Selected for entry, she went on to win the contest at London's Palladium. If Pett needed any endorsement of the choice of his Jane, then this was it.

In a sense, Chrystabel's modelling of Jane was hidden behind a degree of anonymity during the early days of her career. Certainly, in those first couple of years of the new Jane cartoon, there was no exposure to the public as to identities of the artist's life models. Indeed, it is likely that the average reader neither knew nor even cared that life models for Jane existed, much less who they were. For their part, the *Daily Mirror* held no interest in an insignificant model. All told, this was probably just as well.

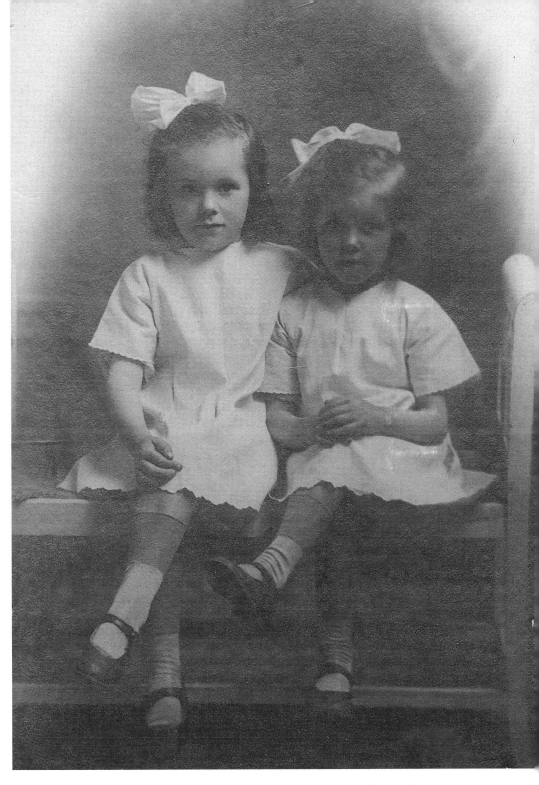

Born on 11 April 1913, Chrystabel Drury is pictured here (right) in about 1916 with her twin sister Sylvia. Chrystabel, already a pretty little girl, would grow up to become the personification of Norman Pett's Jane. She was one of a family of eleven children, of whom only eight survived childhood or infancy.

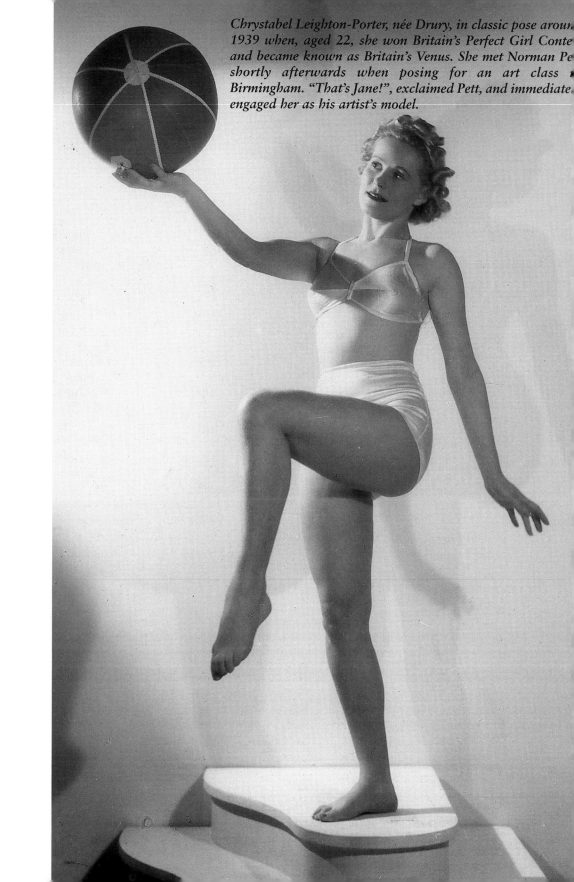

Chrystabel Leighton-Porter, née Drury, in classic pose aroun[d]
1939 when, aged 22, she won Britain's Perfect Girl Conte[st]
and became known as Britain's Venus. She met Norman Pe[tt]
shortly afterwards when posing for an art class [in]
Birmingham. "That's Jane!", exclaimed Pett, and immediate[ly]
engaged her as his artist's model.

Having taken for herself the title "Britain's Perfect Girl", her photographic champion, the one-time Royal Photographer Bertram Park, then seized upon the opportunity to sell pictures of his protégé to various body-beautiful publications. The magazine *Health & Strength* featured various swimsuit-clad poses in its July 1939 edition, identifying her as 22 year-old Miss Chrystabel Leighton-Porter and telling its readers that she had also been voted "Miss Venus of Kent". Another magazine, quite probably *Health & Efficiency*, displayed her in all her glory sitting on a seaside rock and named simply as "Neptune's Daughter". Again, the photographer was Bertram Park. If Pett knew, and he almost certainly did, then he certainly wasn't letting on to his masters at the *Daily Mirror* that his model was posing in the altogether. After all, it was none of their business and all they really cared about was getting their cartoons which, already, were mounting hugely in popularity with the British public at large. Although attitudes in Britain were changing, and changed even faster upon the outbreak of war, there was still more than a degree of disapproval about total (or even partial!) nudity, however tasteful it might be, even within a progressive newspaper like the *Daily Mirror*. It is unlikely that Bartholomew would have wholly approved, and it was not until some years into the war that Chrystabel was first officially introduced to *Daily Mirror* readers as Jane's life model. Interestingly, she was described as Miss Leighton-Porter, still aged just 22, and thus initiating the double subterfuge that was to endure for more than sixty years! However, before then and as early as 1939, when Chrystabel was living for a time in Rochester, Kent, there were those who claimed to have known exactly who she was. Isabelle Diss, then a young lady of approximately the same age as Chrystabel, recalled:

"We lived just across the road then from Chrystabel and we knew exactly who she was. It wasn't any secret and we all knew her simply as Jane. I don't think I knew her by anything else. She was a lovely girl though, so ordinary and always very pleasant and chatty. Her undoubted fame never went to her head and I always thought how odd it was that someone in the public eye seemed to live an almost ordinary life in an ordinary house. I always recall, even with wartime shortages, how well turned out she always was. I mean, the best and the most stylish clothes and hair always perfect. Not for her the Bisto stained legs with painted-in "seams" that we all had to have. Oh no! She had the real thing, silk as well. She turned more than a few heads, I can tell you, and I was always sure that everyone must know who she was!"

But fortunately, then, not everyone did know.

The reality of Pett meeting Jane as an artist's nude life model was carefully hidden from the readership of the *Daily Mirror* when her existence was finally revealed. Instead, for the purpose of a story for

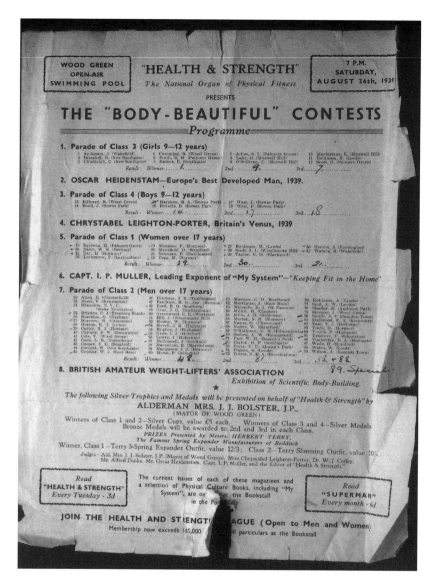

Popular for appearances at Body Beautiful contests and displays, Chrystabel was in demand countrywide. In this programme she appeared at Wood Green just one week before the outbreak of war.

public consumption, Chrystabel had become the telephone operator and receptionist in a Birmingham Hotel when Pett first met her. Most certainly, Chrystabel had never been employed in any such capacity – but it was a useful and decently acceptable cover. At this stage there was not even the remotest hint or suggestion that the modelling was done in the nude. Without a doubt then, it can be seen that it had surely been fortunate the birthday-suited Chrystabel Leighton-Porter, of assorted health and naturist publications, had initially kept quiet about her connections with Jane – albeit that they were still relatively tenuous at that time. In any event, the widespread concept of Jane as a real living person was, then, still some three or more years away although, even as late as 1945, one journalist was having none of it, writing:

> *"Pett automatically calls all his models Jane, a fact which may have lent credence to the popular, and quite inaccurate, public conception that there is a real girl behind the strip."*

Chrystabel's early nude work was for the camera of Bertram Park, although she did not appear as Jane. In this pose, published in 1939, the picture was simply captioned "Neptune's Daughter".

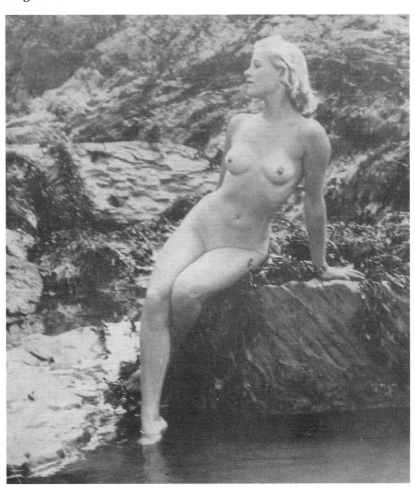

Nonetheless, the idea of Jane as a living, breathing person would develop more by chance than by any intention or design. As Chrystabel later explained, it developed simply through her Jane connections becoming more widely known just as she began a series of unrelated theatrical appearances in 1940 and early 1941.

Chrystabel, aside from her interest in modelling, had already begun to carve out something of a modest career in the theatre. In reality, it was her first love. Modelling was secondary. As a child she had attended the Wimbledon Dancing School, and it was from here that the Mulholland Stage Company engaged her as one of the Babes in pantomime at The Wimbledon Theatre. She adored it, and already knew that show business in one form or another was to be her life. To the delight of her mother, the Mulhollands described her as "the perfect girl" – although that same plaudit, in later years, was apparently not to be quite so joyfully welcomed by her. Moving on into 1939, and the first Christmas of the war, the young Chrystabel was again in panto at The Wimbledon Theatre. Here, she was a dancer in Cinderella and the local *Merton & Morden News* of 8 December 1939 described the cast, and: "… one beauteous little lady who has won the Britain's Perfect Woman contest, Christabel (sic) Leighton-Porter". But no mention, yet, of Jane!

When war had been declared on 3 September 1939 it was, aside from radio announcements, the daily newspapers of Monday 4 September that carried the grim news. Amongst them, of course, the *Daily Mirror*. In that edition, Pett's Jane lightened the gloom with her irrepressible antics. The mere outbreak of a world war didn't stop Jane, and the nation probably needed the continuance of normality and some light-hearted relief to lift the overwhelming sense of foreboding. That day, 4 September '39, and modelled by Chrystabel, our nubile heroine found herself bikini-clad and ready for a beach show. Each frame had been drawn from life by Pett, Chrystabel striking each pose for the artist's pen and pencil. And so it was for all of the cartoons. Six days a week, four frames per strip, and almost all of them drawn from life out of Chrystabel's poses. Archived sketches, though, by the hundred, were hurriedly drawn and filed away by Pett at his Birmingham studio when Chrystabel moved back down to the south of England, although not by any means was this to be the end of the professional relationship. The Jane strip of 4 September 1939 had set the scene for its style throughout the rest of the war though, and not for nothing did the cartoon earn itself the title "the strip that teased!" Scantily clad, clothes askew, skirts ripped and legs-akimbo was very much the continuing Jane style. But never *entirely* naked, and certainly not full frontal. Not, that is, until very much later – and we shall eventually see the interesting significance of the date upon which that momentous event was to occur.

Missing from most of those September 1939 cartoons though, was Jane's faithful companion, the little Dachshund dog. Originally Count

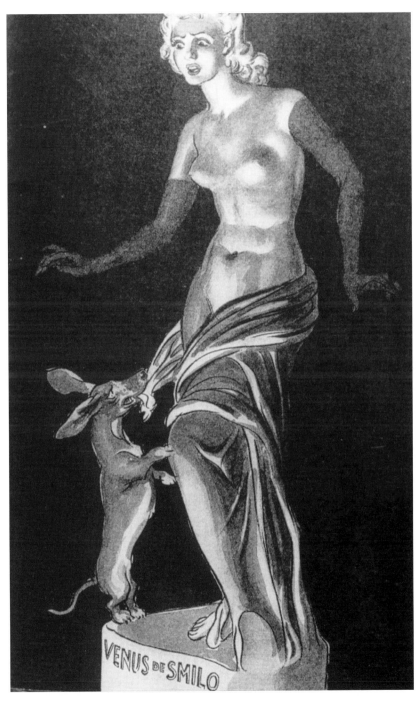

Pett portrays Jane as Venus de Smilo, a pun on both the famous sculpture and Chrystabel's pre-war title of Miss Venus.

Otto von Pumpernickel (Otto for short!) in the Bright Young Thing strip, the dog had now become Fritz. Cautious about anti-German sensitivity amongst its readers, the *Daily Mirror* instructed that poor little Fritz be written out of the script. And so he was. Fritz was sent off to the country, and interned in kennels for the duration! That, however, did not last for long. By early 1940 he was back, the *Mirror* and Freeman recognising that he could easily be turned into a figure of anti-Nazi fun. His return ultimately made the most of national sentiments of the day, with Jane discussing how she wanted to see her Fritz who was still unhappily interned. Overhearing the conversation, a Police Officer asks Jane if she might be talking about a German prisoner.

"*Of course*", she innocently replies, "*but he's a friendly alien!*" Indignant, Jane is seen driving to the internment camp (kennels!) with thought bubbles – "*Fancy that young police officer thinking Fritz was a German – he was born and bred in England!*" The point had clearly been made to the readership, but poking fun at the Germans through Fritz was then acceptably reinforced by the kennel maid who referred to him as "*... our little Nazi – we've been teaching him to Heil Hitler!*" So, Fritz was reinstated. Like Jane, he too was modelled on the real thing, the Petts being keen enthusiasts of the Dachshund breed. From now on, and whenever Jane was drawn, Fritz was inevitably there as well!

For Chrystabel there was work aplenty posing for Norman Pett. At his Moseley, Birmingham, home he sketched Chrystabel prolifically with many of the poses for specific story lines. Others were archived and filed for future use, and Chrystabel recalled, for example, car-driving shots posed sitting on a dining room chair and holding a dustbin lid as a prop for the steering wheel, or a table leg doubling for a telescope in a nautical pose. However, it is important to dispel the myth that Chrystabel was *the* Jane cartoon model. There were others as has already been intimated. For example, Betty Morton who featured in a later photo-shoot for *Picture Post* when she was photographed with Fritz the Dachshund along with the caption: "*A succession of models work hard to maintain the illusion that Jane is a creature of flesh-and-blood and real silk*". The article would have the reader believe that there were many more than just a few Jane models. Indeed, it even suggests that Pett routinely used one model for the top half and another for the bottom half of the Jane figure. Another lovely who appeared briefly on the scene was Joanna Jopson. Although not a blonde she caught the eye and was, however briefly, Jane. Also featuring at some stage in the Jane story was Pett's secretary, Dora Keays. It was she who received from the Parachute Regiment a set of parachutists qualifying "wings", so impressed were the Paras by Jane's somewhat undignified parachute descent in one of the comic strips. Whatever the real truth about the models Pett used, there was only one Jane ... and, of course, only one Chrystabel!

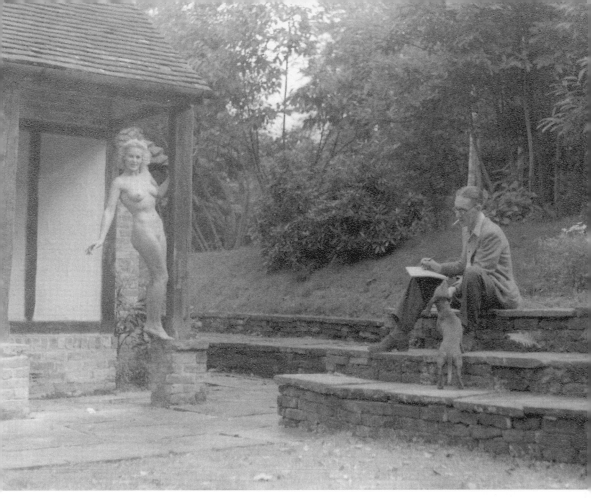

At first, Chrystabel was apprehensive about posing for Norman Pett in the nude but was put at her ease by Mary Pett, Norman's wife. All of the drawings were done in the nude, and every pose for every cartoon frame was drawn from life. Here, Chrystabel poses for Pett in the garden of his Crawley home as Jane's dog, Fritzi the Dachshund, looks on.

As the Battle of Britain unfolded above southern England during the summer of 1940, so Jane continued to be unfolded from the *Daily Mirror* each and every morning. RAF fighter pilot Flt Lt Ian "Widge" Gleed was a particular fan. In his book *Arise to Conquer* (Victor Gollancz Ltd, 1942) Gleed writes of the start of his daily routine on 87 Squadron where he served as a Hurricane pilot.

"We have a quick shave – I cut myself with Dennis' darned sharp razor. Then into the restaurant, which overlooks the 'drome, for a damned good breakfast of bacon and eggs, coffee, toast and marmalade. What's Jane doing this morning? Has she any clothes on today?"

Later, he talks of the loss in combat of his close friend and Commanding Officer of 87 Squadron, New Zealander Squadron Leader Terence Lovell Gregg shot down over Dorset on 15 August 1940. "Shuvvel", as he was affectionately known, was another keen Jane fan and was laid to rest by his comrades in Warmwell parish churchyard. The events a day after his death are recounted by Gleed:

> "We dash into breakfast. "What's Jane doing today? Has she any clothes on?" We peer over Dickie's shoulder; he always buys the Daily Mirror. Bacon and eggs arrive. We eat quickly and in silence. Our papers' headlines all proclaim of the big blitz yesterday. I suppose we are quietly thinking of Shuvvel and Dennis who aren't with us to look at Jane and laugh with us. We don't mention that at all."

The reality of war had hit Gleed and the rest of 87 Squadron hard. Even in the face of death they could still laugh at Jane. Doubtless, they had to. These accounts, perhaps more than any other, signify the importance of Jane to Britain's fighting men. She was still only a cartoon, and yet the part she played in boosting morale had already clearly become inestimable – very often when morale was at its lowest ebb.

As the Battle of Britain proceeded into the Blitz, so Jane continued to lift spirits. Her adventures often reflected topical events in some lighthearted way. Sometimes she would be a Land Army girl, an ATS driver or a munitions factory girl. Whatever, the story line was mostly predictable – it would always end happily, and Jane would, along the way, have shed or lost her clothes, and boyfriend Georgie would still be kept waiting and hoping! Unlike the earlier Bright Young Thing strips, Pett no longer wrote the storylines. These were now the domain of writer John H G "Don" Freeman who had also written the Pip, Squeak & Wilfred cartoons with considerable success and flair, and whom Pett now called his OC Comic Strips. Between them, Pett and Freeman dreamed up storylines that would get Jane in the altogether, or somewhere in that vicinity. It was a somewhat surreal job, often conducted at "conferences" in pubs around the blitzed Fleet Street district and sometimes in the midst of air raids. The venue was usually The White Swan, in the back alleys between Fleet Street and the River Thames. This was the meeting place, a club almost, of all the great cartoon artists of the day: Lunt Roberts, Illingworth, Leo Dowd, Rowland Davies and Giles amongst others. It was here that story boards and drawings were dreamt up over pints of stout, mild and bitter or copious quantities of Scotch! As Freeman later put it:

> "We must have had the best jobs in Britain, Norman and I. Our whole purpose in life, our raison d'etre, was to think up ridiculous ways in which to get the clothes off a gorgeous woman; in fact, the

woman who was probably desired by the majority of red-blooded males in the entire world! And, the best bit of it was that we were getting paid for it as well! Handsomely, too." "But", he added, "as far as the war goes, I'd like to think we did our bit."

And even Pett was equally forthcoming about the financial success their creation had brought them both:

"*I make more money* (out of Jane) *than the Chancellor of the Exchequer collects in taxes*", he once said. "*Only his idea was better. He invented Income Tax, but I think my idea was much more fun*".

As for the *Daily Mirror*, they too were coining in the profits and reaping the benefits of over two million readers a day – many of them certainly driven by a desire to follow Jane. As for Chrystabel, her financial rewards were apparently rather more modest. Sitting fees were paid directly by Pett, and no contract existed between either model and artist or even artist and newspaper. That said, and unknowingly at the time, if not her bank balance then at least Chrystabel's personal life and career would be changed forever by the untold success of Jane.

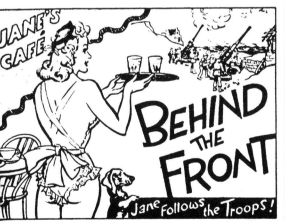 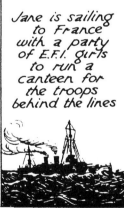 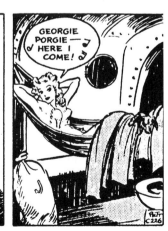

Chapter Two

The Early Years: Blitzy and Fritzi

The Battle of France, the Battle of Britain, the Blitz, Battle of The Atlantic and El Alamein. Throughout them all Pett's Jane had sustained the troops and cheered civilians back home. Interestingly, the appeal of Jane was not entirely exclusive to the male population. At the time this book is being written the content of the wartime Jane cartoons would be thought of as somewhat banal – not to mention sexist and certainly exploitative of women. What the feminist movement would today make of it is not hard to imagine, but in the world of the 1940s its acceptance was universal by both sexes. The newspaper itself conducted a survey that identified that 82% of its women readers looked at Jane, as against 71% of the men readers. Newsprint shortages, or the Blitz, though, had sometimes meant the *Daily Mirror* and Jane would be in short supply, or even not available at all. When that happened, noted one commentator, there were rather a lot of unhappy faces. It was certainly a strange thing, and became very much a part of the inexplicable phenomenon that was Jane, but *no* Jane often equalled *no* spirit among the services in particular. But was this really an inexplicable phenomenon? *"I used to wonder"*, said Chrystabel, *"what <u>was</u> the big attraction? Then, just the other day, someone said to me – don't be so silly, it was sex! I would have been truly horrified if I'd ever known or even thought that! It never really occurred to me."* Little wonder, then, that the armed forces were sometimes referred to as "Jane's fighting men" – even once, or so it is claimed, in Parliament!

The War Office were not slow in recognising Jane's importance to the armed services, and before very long – especially as British forces were now spread widely around the globe – the Jane strip cartoons were being syndicated to a variety of Army, Navy and Air Force publications and a selection of other overseas newspapers as well. Amongst them, for example, was the *Eighth Army News* where Jane appeared, in each edition, across the bottom of the back page. These were merely repeats of the cartoons already run in the *Daily Mirror* back home, not newly commissioned cartoons. Significantly, no other cartoons were carried in this particular newspaper, and so it was for the other similar news-sheets that featured our dizzy blonde. It all served to boost and reinforce Jane's growing popularity. For the Canadians, there was *Over Seas* for whom Pett drew a saucy Jane called Maple Sugar, but with strategic maple leaves positioned where the fig leaves traditionally went! Other venues

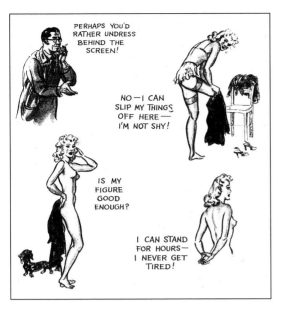

PERHAPS YOU'D
RATHER UNDRESS
BEHIND THE
SCREEN!

NO — I CAN
SLIP MY THINGS
OFF HERE —
I'M NOT SHY!

IS MY
FIGURE
GOOD
ENOUGH?

I CAN STAND
FOR HOURS —
I NEVER GET
TIRED!

To mark Chrystabel's first sitting, Pett executed this set of four sketches to include a self portrait of the artist. These are classic Jane poses, although total nudity like this did not creep into the cartoons until June 1944.

for Jane were *Gunpit* and *Union Jack*, again the cartoon strips being printed on the bottom of each back page. But for many a home-sick or Jane-sick trooper, packages from home would be sent containing bundles of Jane cuttings. It is quite possible that the reason a majority of Jane readers were women was simply that they were collecting the cartoons to send to their absent menfolk! Whatever, the saying that "The war can wait – what's Jane been up to?" was certainly true for thousands whose daily routine began with Jane. The importance of Jane in apparently continuing with this war had been firmly established. And therein lay a problem.

By nature, Pett was an industrious fellow, but a gregarious one as well. Often, he would work well into the wee small hours at his drawing board or easel, inking in or putting the finishing touches to a strip. However, should any friend, neighbour or acquaintance just happen to be passing by, as was very often the case … then here was the perfect excuse he needed to down pen and pencil and break open the Scotch. As Chrystabel later put it, he was a party animal. Sometimes, Jane could wait. That, however, did not please the *Daily Mirror* and his tardiness became an increasingly difficult problem for the editorial staff and cartoon editor up in London. Ultimately, the newspaper pulled the plug. Jane, they decided, was no more. If Hitler had turned up living in a Bexhill seafront Guest House along with Vera Lynn then it could not have created more of a sensational or newsworthy stir than did the demise of Jane. Across the length and breadth of Britain, from Paddington Railway Station to the tiny Dorset village of Ansty, the funny little Mr Chad character peering out over his tiny fence was chalked on walls and bridges. "Wot!? No Jane?" read the accompanying graffiti. Something had to be done. Inundated with countless 'phone calls, visitors, telegrams and letters, the *Daily Mirror* heartily agreed. Plummeting sales had also, no doubt, focused collective executive minds.

Together, the *Daily Mirror* and Pett hatched a plan. Pett would produce a cartoon to tell the readers that Jane would be back. In return, the *Daily Mirror* would reinstate Pett as the Jane artist provided that he

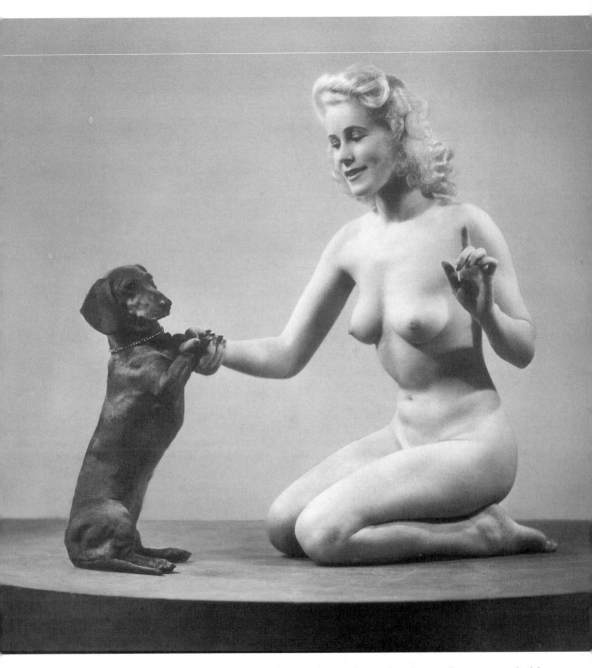

Little Fritzi is encourgaed to sit and beg in this nude study of Jane that was probably produced for Jane's Journal and to be sold, commercially, as a print for Jane fans.

18

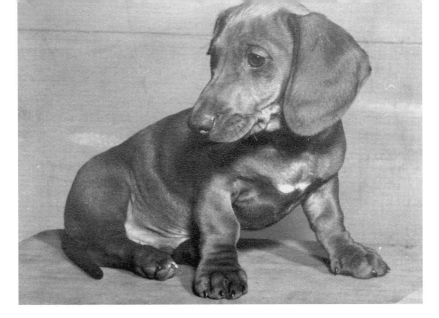

Fritzi, Jane's little dog, was an essential part of the Jane storyline. A family pet belonging to Norman and Mary, Fritzi was temporarily written out of the script during the early part of the war for fear of inflaming anti-German feelings! In the end, he was used to poke fun at the Nazis. Later, the dog would appear in the Jane stage shows, although there were several Fritzis before both the cartoons and the stage shows had run their course.

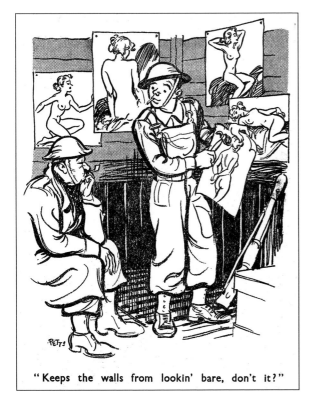

"Keeps the walls from lookin' bare, don't it?"

undertook in future to continually supply the cartoons up to six weeks in advance. Pett agreed, and for Chrystabel it meant the end of her chore of rushing to the railway station to put the most recent drawings on the last train up to London for tomorrow's newspaper. Norman's plan for the return of Jane was simple, and utterly inkeeping with the character's type. In a single box stood Jane, all but bereft of her clothes, and

Pett had been an infantryman during the First World War and so understood the soldier's keen interest in the pin-up girl, the famous Kirchner girl being the object of the Tommies' desire in the trenches of France and Belgium. This was his personal 1940 Christmas card, prophetically illustrating the up-and-coming popularity of his creation, Jane, with the armed forces.

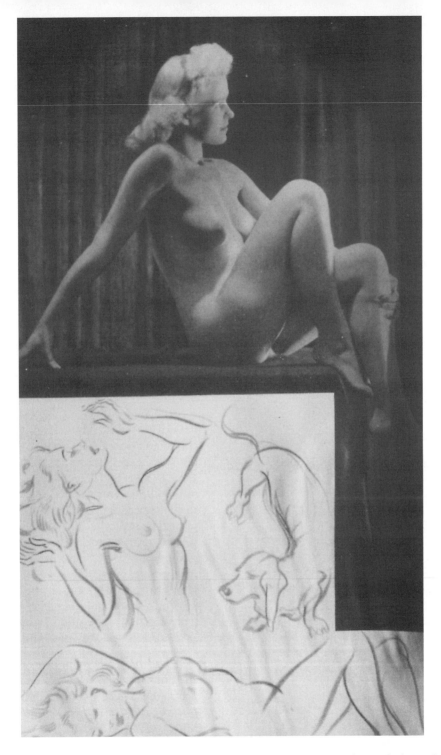

Examples of Pett's working sketches of Jane drawn using Chrystabel Leighton-Porter as the life model – and Fritzi as himself – shown with a typical Jane pose. However, the nature of these poses make it more than likely that these were drawn as pin-ups for the later Jane's Journal rather than as cartoons. Nevertheless, hundreds of similar drawings were made by Pett and filed away for reference and eventual use.

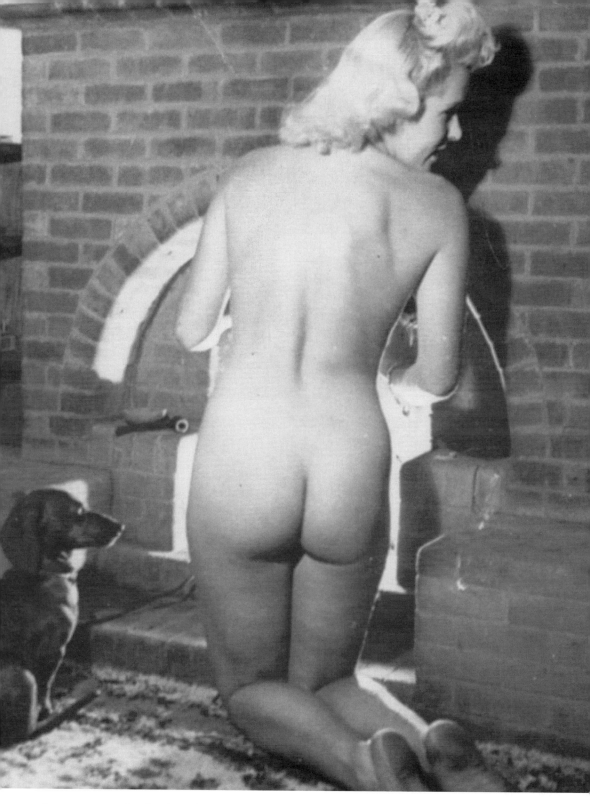

Jane gets cosy by the fireside in Norman Pett's house during one of her almost daily sitting sessions for the cartoon or Journal.

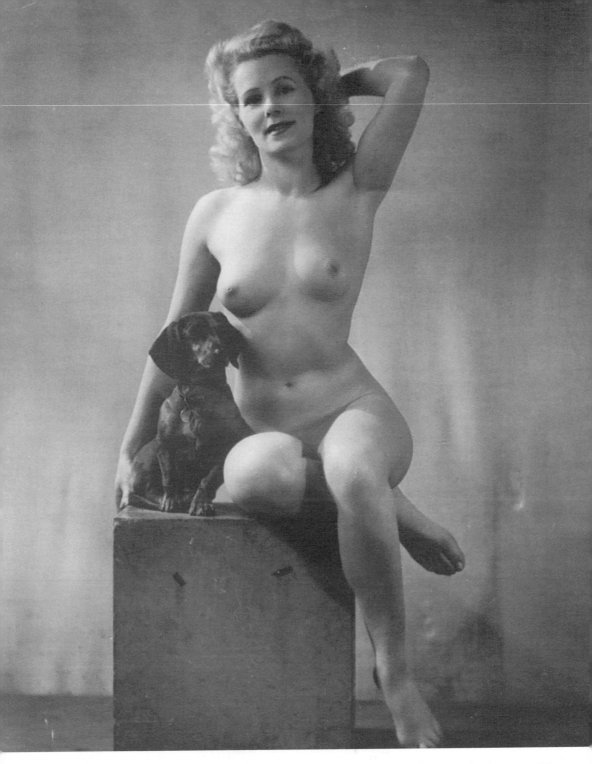

Jane in all her glory poses for Bertram Park's camera in another popular image sold to Jane fans. There must have been countless hundreds of pictures like this, signed and dedicated by Jane, that were treasured possessions of servicemen. Probably but few survived – having been dumped by the original owners upon returning home from the war and fearful of the ire of wives and girlfriends!

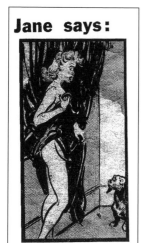

Jane says:

"In reply to all your many inquiries as to what has happened to me! Give me a break. I CAN'T FIND MY PANTIES!"

Pett's tardiness in delivering artwork on time often led to problems with his bosses at the Daily Mirror, *with the result that once during the war the newspaper stopped publication of the Jane strip cartoon. An outcry followed, and this was the single cartoon that explained her absence …*

clutching a pair of curtains for the sake of modesty. Beneath her were the words:

"In reply to all your many inquiries as to what has happened to me: Give me a break. I CAN'T FIND MY PANTIES!"

The effect was immediate, and literally quite overwhelming. If the staff at the *Daily Mirror* had been surprised by the response when Jane had initially been dropped, then nothing could have prepared them for what happened next. Fetter Lane was blocked with mail vans and delivery boys – all of them bringing hundreds upon hundreds of letters, most of them containing pairs of undies. The question, of course,

The result, inevitably, was sack-loads of underwear being sent in by readers to the Daily Mirror *and these were then sent on to Pett and Chrystabel. This was one such pair, in silk and lace, that went on to be used by Chrystabel in some of her wartime stage shows and which was still a treasured memento over fifty years later!*

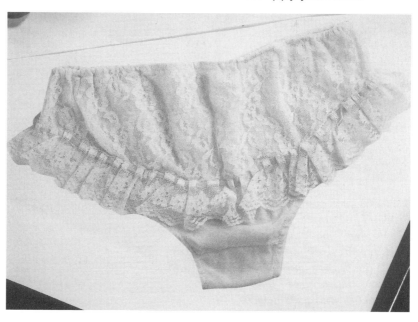

was what to do with them all – but for Chrystabel this was certainly not a problem. As she later pointed out, she was in the theatre with a troupe of chorus girls, dancers and other performers. And, of course, she had eight sisters. With wartime shortages, and clothing available only on a coupon-rationing scheme, these were indeed welcome and unexpected gifts that she collected by the basket-load from the *Mirror* offices over a period of a week or so. As for Chrystabel's Jane, she would certainly not be wanting for panties yet, or for many a long while to come. Frilly ones, lacy ones, silk ones and French ones – but all of them, recalled Chrys, were just her size –

... and this the single cartoon that announced her return!

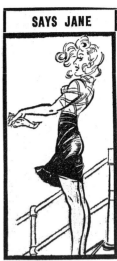

SAYS JANE

Thanks for the letters, telegrams and 'phone calls— and for the panties, safely received. I'll be in action again on Monday, I hope.

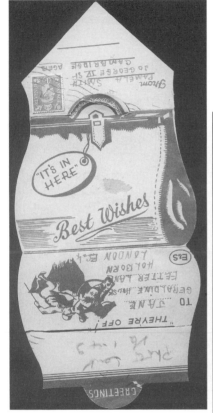

This was the offering of thirteen-year-old Pamela Smith of Cambridge who came to Jane's assistance at the hour of her need. Pett's annotation in red crayon indicates that a signed photo was sent out to young Pamela on 26 January 1943.

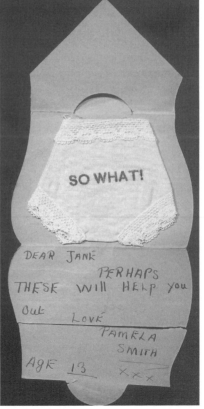

Here is the reverse.

24

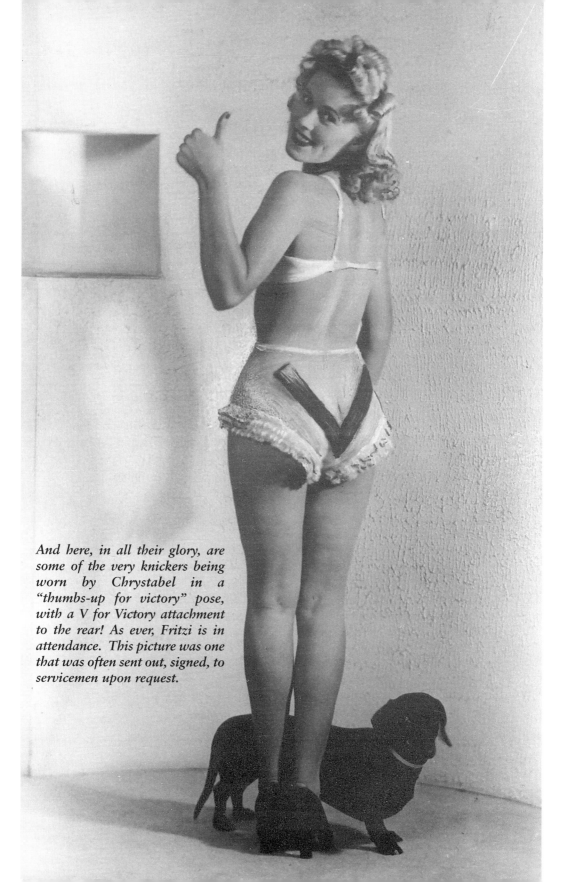

And here, in all their glory, are some of the very knickers being worn by Chrystabel in a "thumbs-up for victory" pose, with a V for Victory attachment to the rear! As ever, Fritzi is in attendance. This picture was one that was often sent out, signed, to servicemen upon request.

that is, bar one! Thirteen- year-old Pamela Smith of Cambridge sent Jane a humorous fold-out greetings card with a miniature pair of silk and lace undies inside, and stamped with the words "So what!" and the hand written message "Hope these will help you out." It was typical of the spontaneous response to the desperate plight of the nation's favourite heroine.

As for some of the letters, messages like *"What! Again?"*, *"She should worry!"*, *"It's never bothered her before"* and *"Come on out and give Georgie a break!"* were typical. In response to the outcry, Pett penned another single cartoon. This time she was fully clothed, if not a little windswept, and standing on a seaside promenade. Beneath her the caption:

> *"Thanks for the letters, telegrams and 'phone calls – and for the panties, safely received. I'll be in action again on Monday, I hope".*

At the point when this second cartoon was published, Pett had not yet produced even the start of the stash of new drawings that had been his part of the reinstatement deal. Consequently, the *Daily Mirror* inserted this cautionary note at the end of the second cartoon's caption. As Norman Pett would later wittily remark: *"I suppose they didn't want to get caught with their pants down for a second time around."*

Fortunately for all concerned, the end of this particular story ended up much like the cartoon strip storyline. Pett managed to meet his agreed deadlines, Jane was saved and everyone was happy. That is, until the storyline took our intrepid heroine closer to marriage with her long-term boyfriend Georgie-Porgie. Then, things took quite another turn.

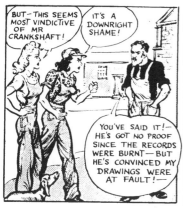

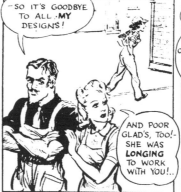

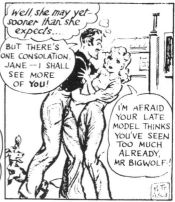

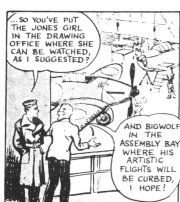

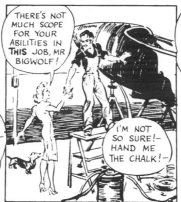

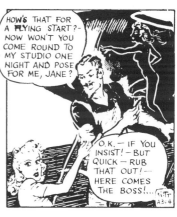

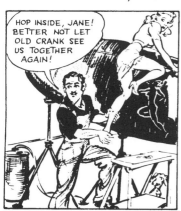

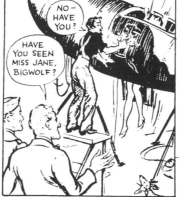

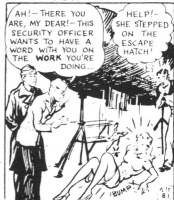

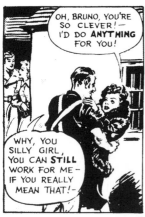

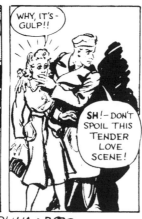

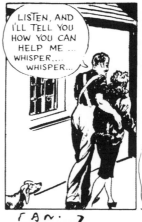

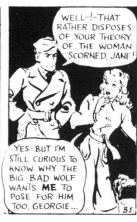

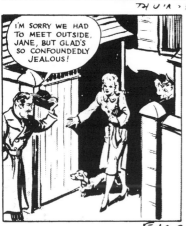

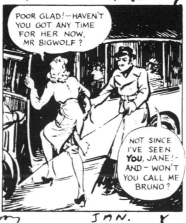

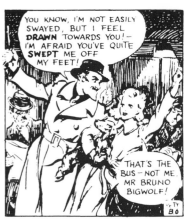

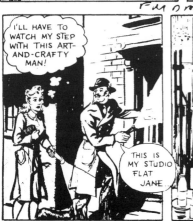

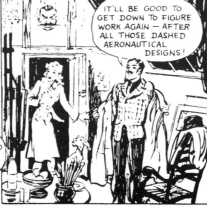

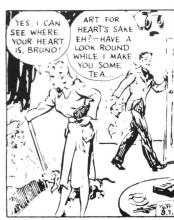

Chapter Three

Marry me, Jane!

For Jane, marriage proposals were two a penny. In fact, and to be absolutely precise about it, in one single week of the war, Jane of the *Daily Mirror* had no less than sixty-two marriage proposals. By 1943 Chrystabel Leighton-Porter had very much become Jane. Her promotion through stage shows and charity appearances, as well as her eventual "outing" in the *Daily Mirror* itself, had made absolutely sure of this. Chrystabel now became a regular visitor to Fetter Lane where she spent hours of each week dealing with correspondence from her fans. Mostly, this was just a case of signing photographs or standard letters to send back to her adoring public. Sometimes, copies of Pett drawings were duly signed and sent out. Other times it would be signed photographs, but mostly these were nothing more provocative than head and shoulder portrait shots. All of this adulation convinced the *Daily Mirror*, Pett and Chrystabel herself that Jane could not be married off. Jane was everyone's girlfriend, and must surely remain so. All the same, Pett and Freeman decided to tease their readership in a storyline that ran through 1943 and on into 1944. Titled "Marriage by Proxy", it led with a box showing an airman, a soldier and a sailor. Under each were the words: "Why is the RAF raving – the Navy belligerent – the Army fighting mad? Because Jane is going to marry Georgie! OR IS SHE?" In more ways than one, this really was the strip that teased.

Speaking in 1999, Chrystabel told of how that, during the war, she was already secretly married to Arthur, an RAF fighter pilot. The implication had always seemed to be that Chrystabel and Arthur had married at some time during the war, although she never said she *had* and never said she *hadn't* either! Talking about it to the media in the 1980s she said: "I didn't exactly sign any contract to say I wouldn't get married, but it was very clearly understood that anybody could feel they might be my boyfriend. Even now I'm still deliberately vague about my marriage. I would hate my boys to think I had been deceitful." And so, the marriage of Chrystabel – Jane to millions – was possibly the best kept secret of World War Two aside from the plans for D-Day and Enigma. But there was a deeper secret: Chrystabel had *already* married her Arthur, and a long time before she ever became Jane.

Incredibly, Chrystabel and Arthur had been married way back in 1934. This fact, of course, would rather belie the almost perpetual age of 22 at which Chrystabel seemed to be stuck from around the year of 1942. If this age had been correct, then we would have to accept that Jane had perhaps

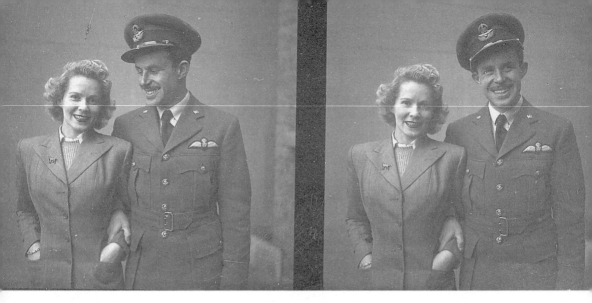

Chrystabel Leighton-Porter and her fighter pilot husband, Arthur, in 1943. A Typhoon pilot, Arthur flew operationally on D-Day – just as Jane the cartoon girl was getting ready to get her clothes off for the very first time.

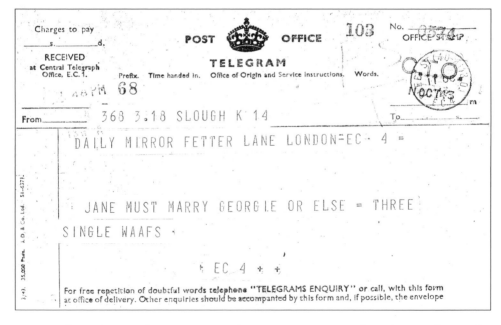

During the 1943 storyline "Marriage by Proxy", a mass of mail poured into the offices of the Daily Mirror on the highly controversial subject of her proposed marriage. Most begged her not to marry, but this was an exception to that rule – a telegram from "Three single WAAFS" insisting the marriage went ahead. Clearly, with Jane married off, these three girls felt the field of competition would be significantly narrowed!

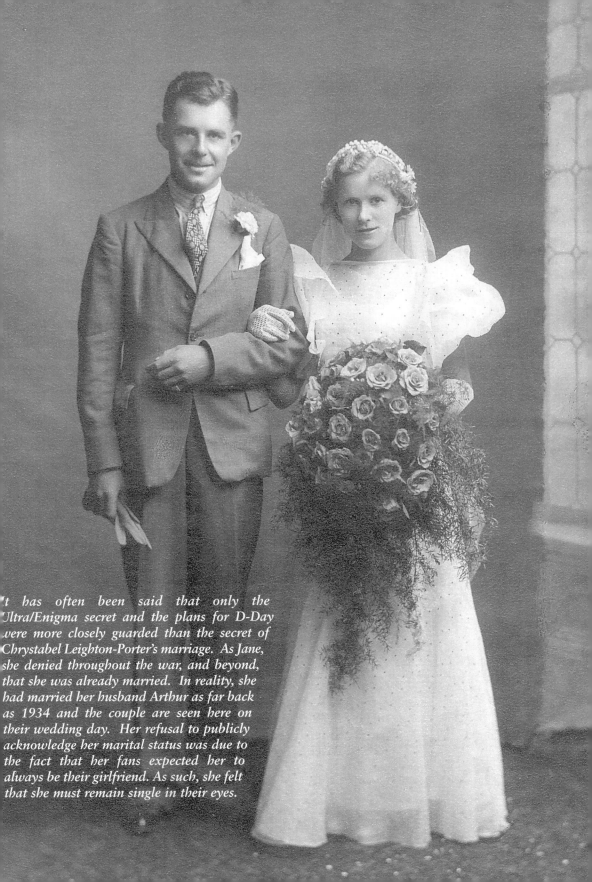

It has often been said that only the Ultra/Enigma secret and the plans for D-Day were more closely guarded than the secret of Chrystabel Leighton-Porter's marriage. As Jane, she denied throughout the war, and beyond, that she was already married. In reality, she had married her husband Arthur as far back as 1934 and the couple are seen here on their wedding day. Her refusal to publicly acknowledge her marital status was due to the fact that her fans expected her to always be their girlfriend. As such, she felt that she must remain single in their eyes.

married at the age of 15 or earlier. Clearly, she hadn't. All the same, the vagueness about age has been an almost timeless traditional show business foible. What artiste of any note has not been 21 for at least three or four years or more, or even slipped back a year or two? No, there was nothing dishonest in the rather grey area of Chrystabel's age. As she herself so succinctly put it: *"Jane is timeless and ageless. And so am I!"* What lady of a certain age would not give anything for an excuse like that? As to the marriage secret, again Chrystabel had merely been deliberately vague. Economical with the facts, perhaps. Later, much later, it would be the media who concluded that she had married during the war. Chrystabel neither confirmed nor denied it. However, the so-called "secret" of her marriage had been perpetrated for the very sound and understandable reason that she did not want to spoil things for her fans. After all, to them she had become Jane and once both of the deceptions had been started it was very difficult for Chrystabel not to ensure their continuance.

Letters from admirers, and proposals (often serious!), continued to flood in throughout the war and in the immediate post-war years, according to Chrystabel, at the rate of dozens each day! Sadly, Chrystabel herself later disposed of most of these letters. In themselves they would have been a fascinating social archive. Most were apparently innocent, and they perhaps fell into the genre of today's fan letters sent by the sack-load to pop musicians and film stars. Some, though, had a slightly more seedy edge to them and one such letter that somehow survived falls into that category. Almost voyeuristic to read, it does perhaps give something of an insight into the extent of the impact that Jane had had upon so many of her followers. It was dated 9 August 1946 and was from a devoted fan living in Handsworth, Birmingham:

Dear Jane,
After seeing your performance at the Astor I think you are the most wonderful girl I have ever seen and I would like very much if you would care to come out with me one evening in my car. If you would come I'd willingly give you £100-00-00 for one beautiful night. If you are interested, write in the first instance to me.
Yours in anticipation,

J.D.

If genuine, and not from a crank, then it illustrates the extent to which some of Jane's followers were besotted. By 1946 standards, one hundred pounds was a fairly considerable sum of money although the underlying nature and intent of this offer is clearly apparent. Such offers, as well as hundreds of rather more innocent ones, were not uncommon. Certainly, the more innocent letters were in the majority and reflected the charm of her character – oozing sex appeal and yet naïvely unaware of it, even if her

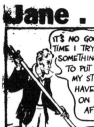
Jane . . .

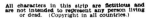

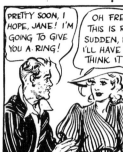

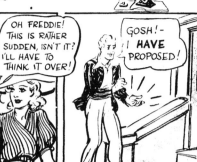

IT'S NO GOOD!—EVERY TIME I TRY TO PROPOSE SOMETHING HAPPENS TO PUT ME OFF MY STROKE!—I'LL HAVE TO DO IT ON THE PHONE AFTER ALL!

THANK YOU FOR A LOVELY DAY, FREDDIE—I'VE ENJOYED EVERY MINUTE OF IT! WHEN SHALL I SEE YOU AGAIN?

PRETTY SOON, I HOPE, JANE! I'M GOING TO GIVE YOU A RING!

OH FREDDIE! THIS IS RATHER SUDDEN, ISN'T IT? I'LL HAVE TO THINK IT OVER!

GOSH!— I HAVE PROPOSED!

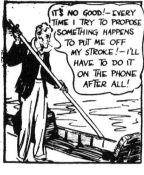
Jane . . .

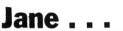

THIS YEAR—NEXT YEAR—SOMETIME, NEVER!

WELL, JANE, DID HE PROPOSE?

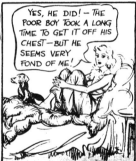

YES, HE DID!—THE POOR BOY TOOK A LONG TIME TO GET IT OFF HIS CHEST—BUT HE SEEMS VERY FOND OF ME!

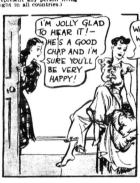

I'M JOLLY GLAD TO HEAR IT!—HE'S A GOOD CHAP, AND I'M SURE YOU'LL BE VERY HAPPY!

WHEN'S THE WEDDING TO BE, JANE?

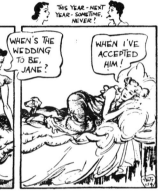

WHEN I'VE ACCEPTED HIM!

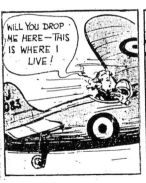

WILL YOU DROP ME HERE—THIS IS WHERE I LIVE!

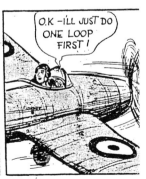

O.K.—I'LL JUST DO ONE LOOP FIRST!

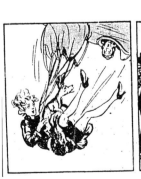

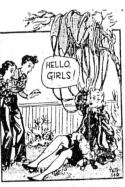

HELLO, GIRLS!

33

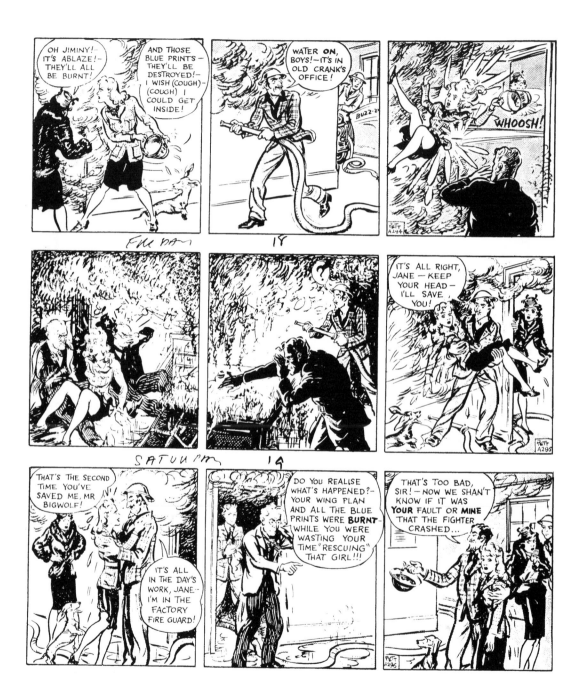

34

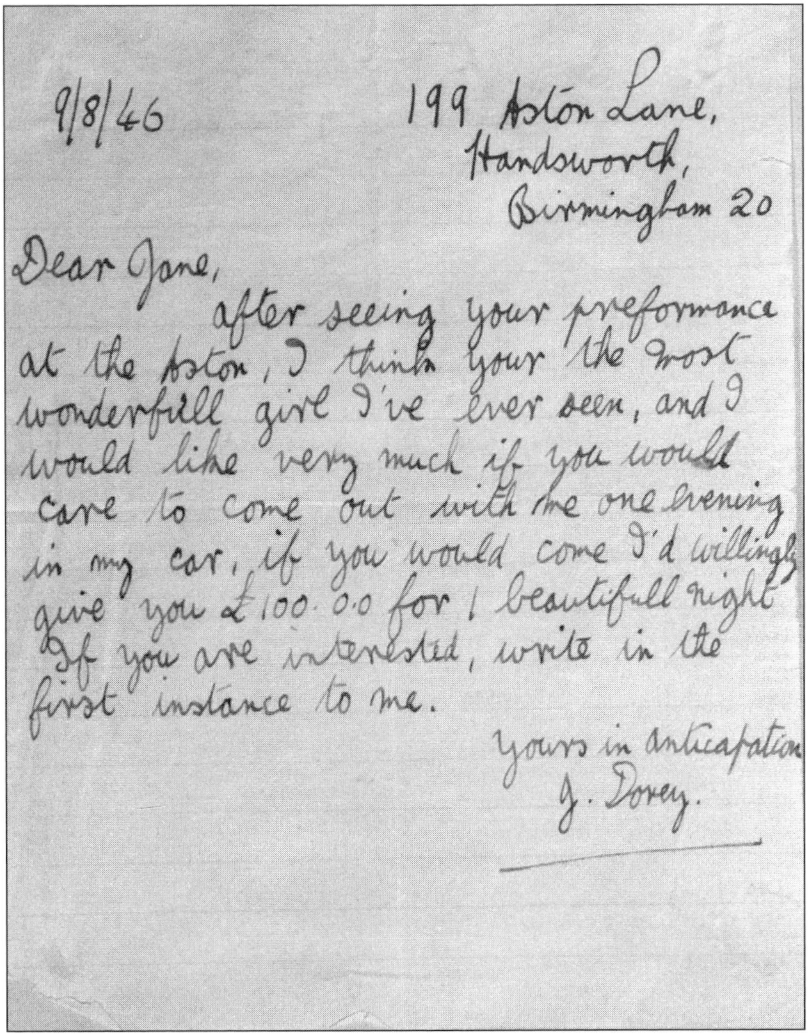

9/8/46

199 Aston Lane,
Handsworth,
Birmingham 20

Dear Jane,
after seeing your preformance at the Aston, I think your the most wonderfull girl I've ever seen, and I would like very much if you would care to come out with me one evening in my car, if you would come I'd willingly give you £100. 0.0 for 1 beautifull night If you are interested, write in the first instance to me.

Yours in anticapation
J. Dorey.

Indecent proposal? Some of the hundreds of proposals that came in were not always of the harmless "Will you marry me?" kind. This example, just post-war, has certain less than savoury undertones. Though not typical, it was not unusual.

admirers were *very* much aware of it! But she was, and remained, a fantasy girl in the literal sense of the word – as unattainable in the flesh as she was in the make-believe-world of the cartoon. Everyone knew that, but it was always possible to dream and Chrystabel was determined that, through her personification of Jane, they could hold onto that dream forever. To the end of her life she somehow felt that she couldn't let her boys down. And she didn't.

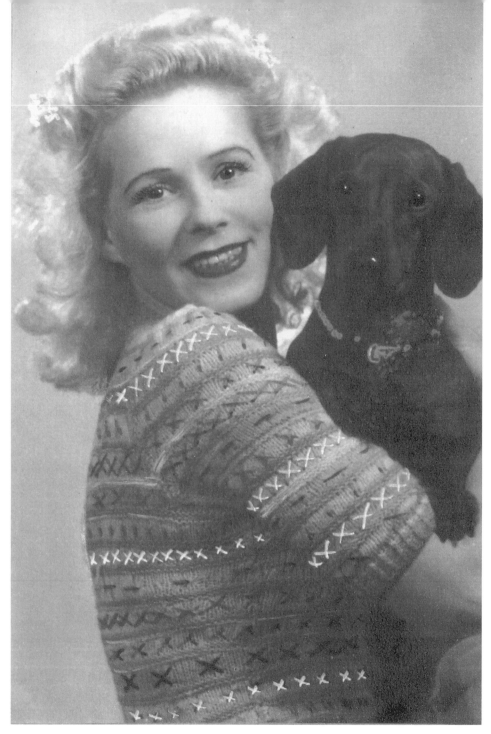

One of the photographs often signed by Chrystabel as Jane and sent out to fans was this homely and inoffensive image of Jane with her Fritzi. Many of her fans were young children, and so the more risqué nude shots were reserved to be sent out only by the Daily Mirror, *and only to servicemen. This shot, however, was very much of the period and portrayed innocent girl-next-door charms. In itself, this particular photograph is said to have prompted dozens of marriage proposals as it idealised her charms as the perfect woman.*

Back to 1943 though, and to the Marriage by Proxy storyline. Here was a tale that ran and ran. Day after day, week after week, Freeman teased and Pett provoked the readers. In outline, the story concerned the proposed marriage of Jane to her long-time boyfriend, Georgie *(who allegedly, according to Chrystabel, was based rather unkindly on Mary Pett's female golfing partner!)* In the event, Georgie is called away on active service but Jane ends up being tricked into believing that she has married him by proxy although, instead, she has actually married her "proxy" husband, the sinister and calculating Colonel Boloney, for real. Freeman gave the story rather more twists and turns than usual, with Pett providing a loss of clothing as a regular occurrence and with the ever present chance that Jane would resolve her predicament of her marriage to Boloney and, finally, marry Georgie. It was an innocent and really quite silly storyline, but it provoked an avalanche of mail. By the thousand, servicemen wrote in begging the storywriters not to let Jane be married off, and one telegram to the *Daily Mirror* is typical. It was dated 11 October 1943, and read: "JANE MUST MARRY GEORGIE OR ELSE. THREE SINGLE WAAFS". Another letter enclosed a cutting of Jane saying "Now what shall I wear for my wedding, Fritz?" Underneath, the sender had implored: "Stay our No 1 Glamour Girl Jane!" Another telegram from a Sgt Major McNeil of the 645th Bty RA, even offered leave (*passionate* leave, the telegram said!) for Georgie in order that he could marry Jane.

By the time the cartoon finally ended, Jane had never married her Georgie. Instead, she just sailed off into the sunset with him! The response though, to the question as to whether Jane should marry or not, told Chrystabel all she needed to know. Her mind was firmly made up over whether she should be open with her fans about her marriage to Arthur.

Chapter Four

Jane on Stage

"The star turn in the new road show, "Jane's Back", staged by Anglo-American Productions, is, of course, the personal appearance of "Jane" the well known cartoon girl of the "Daily Mirror". Jane, a glamorous blonde, introduces herself by stepping from her bath, and then offers a series of art poses. The act, which was received with a good deal of applause, was presented with much artistic skill, Jane being in the centre of a huge circular frame with striking lighting effects"

The *Western Daily Times*, August 1943.

The concept of Jane as a stage show was never even so much as imagined by Norman Pett. Like script writer Freeman, he purposely distanced himself from Jane's various theatrical productions and both of them refused to in any way endorse any of the shows. Similarly, and contrary to popular belief, the *Daily Mirror* never promoted or formally approved of Chrystabel's live shows and even went so far as to publicly state that there was no "official" Jane. But that is not to say that Pett, Freeman or the *Mirror* were actually displeased about the thespian direction of Chrystabel's Jane, and neither did they discourage her treading the boards. It all added to what, to use the current idiom, would be called the hype. In effect, this was a symbiotic relationship where the *Daily Mirror* gained additional useful free promotion, the public increased its thirst for Jane and demanded more of the same – to the benefit of Pett and Freeman – whilst Chrystabel herself further established a place as Pett's favoured model at the same time generating a thirst for more live shows. Everyone was happy, although it was almost certainly due largely to the Ministry of Labour and ENSA turning a very deliberate blind eye that enabled Chrystabel Leighton-Porter to pursue a career as, what she called, the "official unofficial Jane".

As early as September 1939, the noted theatrical producer and manager, Basil Dean, set up The Entertainments National Service Association – ENSA for short. Its brief was simple and set out in an official press release which read:

"The organisation for the provision of entertainments for His Majesty's Forces both at home and abroad is now completed. The Navy, Army and Air Force Institutes will be responsible for the organisation, control and finance of the entertainments. ENSA will provide the entertainment asked for through various committees. The entertainments are scheduled to begin on Monday week, September 25 1939."

Almost immediately, actors were required to register with ENSA. Failure to do so would result in the actor or actress being called up for some form of national service – either in the military, in factories, farms, mines or elsewhere. Registration with ENSA meant that the artiste undertook to be available for at least six weeks in any year for official entertainments. For Chrystabel, having appeared on stage soon after the inception of ENSA, she was required to sign up and consequently did so. Having registered, she was exempted from any other form of service unless her circumstances changed, and remained "on call" for the duration of hostilities. Nevertheless, she was never called up for a single ENSA performance. Chrystabel explained why:

> "I think they felt that my show was a little too risqué, and perhaps risky, to put on for a theatre full of lusty troops! It was a different matter when I did stage shows in provincial theatres, because although there were always a lot of the boys there, there were always lots of the general public too. As well, it was in a slightly more controlled environment really. It was really all quite orderly, although once the Police had to protect me, and the glass screens holding my pictures at the front of house were often broken by souvenir hunters intent on getting a photo. So, all things considered, I suppose things could have got out of hand if it were just a couple of hundred or so servicemen on an army base somewhere! As it happened, and although lots of the troops came to all of my shows, there was never even a hint of real trouble with them. They were lovely. Anyway, although ENSA never called me I remained on their books and, in theory, could have been called up at any time. So that was that, and it meant I didn't get called up for any other war service which would have otherwise stopped my stage career or modelling work."

Maybe, and although ENSA probably never had any intention of calling her, she was "kept on the books" and a blind eye simply turned so as to enable her to continue in her own direction. Most certainly the powers that be would have recognised Jane's importance to national morale – whether as part of ENSA or not. In reality, ENSA had more of an image that suited the darling and appealing Vera Lynn – rather than the daring and revealing Jane!

Vera Lynn of course was the Forces' Sweetheart, but Jane was certainly their undisputed pin-up. As Chrystabel herself put it, "Vera Lynn was the voice of World War Two, but I was the body!" And naturally it was that particular body with its famous curves and long

Chrystabel first trod the boards in pantomime at the Wimbledon Theatre in December 1939, just after the outbreak of war, although she did not appear as Jane and did not yet appear on the billing.

shapely legs that drew the crowds to her stage shows. Singing was not her forté, although, as we shall see, one particular song did become a regular feature of the usual show.

After pantomime at Wimbledon in 1940, the promotion of Jane on stage took on a new lease of life, although it was largely through her achievement as Britain's Perfect Girl rather than as Jane that ensured her first stage work. In early 1941, Chrystabel Leighton-Porter was signed up to appear in what was billed as an "American-Style Revue" called Hi-Diddle-Diddle and touring various UK theatres. At this time, however, there was

From mid-1941, Chrystabel Leighton-Porter appeared as Jane in the Anglo-American stage production Hi-Diddle-Diddle and appeared at a variety of UK venues including the Theatre Royal, Lincoln, and the Empire.

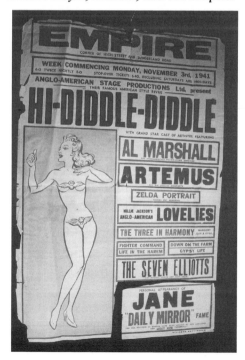

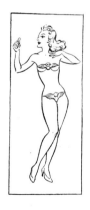

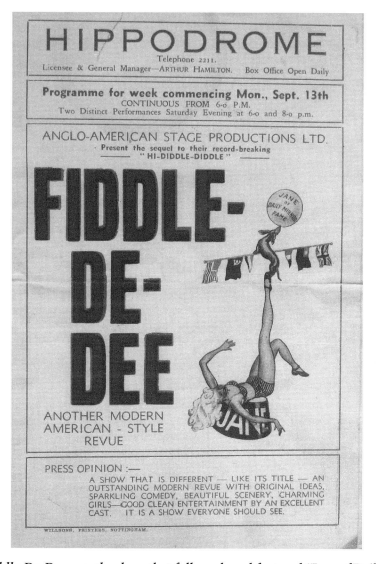

HIPPODROME

Telephone 2211.

Licensee & General Manager—ARTHUR HAMILTON.   Box Office Open Daily

Programme for week commencing Mon., Sept. 13th
CONTINUOUS FROM 6-0 P.M.
Two Distinct Performances Saturday Evening at 6-0 and 8-0 p.m.

ANGLO-AMERICAN STAGE PRODUCTIONS LTD.
Present the sequel to their record-breaking
——— " HI-DIDDLE-DIDDLE " ———

FIDDLE-DE-DEE

ANOTHER MODERN
AMERICAN - STYLE
REVUE

PRESS OPINION :—
A SHOW THAT IS DIFFERENT — LIKE ITS TITLE — AN
OUTSTANDING MODERN REVUE WITH ORIGINAL IDEAS,
SPARKLING COMEDY, BEAUTIFUL SCENERY, CHARMING
GIRLS—GOOD CLEAN ENTERTAINMENT BY AN EXCELLENT
CAST.   IT IS A SHOW EVERYONE SHOULD SEE.

WILLSONS, PRINTERS, NOTTINGHAM.

Fiddle-De-Dee was the show that followed, and featured "Jane of Daily Mirror Fame" prominently in its billing – although the Daily Mirror and Norman Pett would never officially endorse the Jane stage shows. Nevertheless, they turned a blind eye to what amounted to a generous helping of free publicity.

no link to Jane as such, although the theatre bills did depict a very similar Jane-like figure. The same production company, Anglo-American Stage Productions Ltd, followed on very shortly with that particular show's successor, called Fiddle-De-Dee. This time, Jane featured prominently on the front cover of the programme as well as on the inside and on the back cover, where she was described as "Jane of *Daily Mirror* Fame". Newspaper reviews described "Fiddle-De-Dee" at the Savoy Theatre, Scunthorpe, as a show that comprised Jane singing "In the blue of the evening", and numbers by Al Marshall, Vicki Cowan and the Loretta Dancers. Bizarrely, if not topically, the show also contained "*… an air combat in ballet with a darting Spitfire mowing down Messerschmitts in a feature of smart chorus work.*" This was probably the first time that any direct link with Jane had been made. Initially, these shows had been purely variety and included the usual mix of comedians, musicians and dancers, although it was not long before Jane's act developed into what would be described as a *tableaux vivant* act. For its day it was nothing short of daring.

During this period it was strictly prohibited for nudes to move on stage (see also Chapter 5: Of Nudes and Prudes) and thus the only possibility was the *tableaux* presentation. Laurie Pink was a stagehand at The Empire, Bristol, and told how the show worked behind the scenes. He reckoned that he had the best job in Britain when Jane came to his theatre!

"One week I was informed that we would be having the one and only Jane doing her act. She would be in the nude except for small pieces of silk in all the right places. Great! But alas we were then told that during the act all hands would be ordered off the stage and out of the wings. My heart sank. To think that for all those years I had enjoyed Jane in the Daily Mirror *and now she was here in the flesh I was forbidden to see her act. I was devastated. On the day Jane arrived at the theatre she was the centre of attention. Then, just before her act started, I was called over by the Stage Manager and told that I was to assist Jane during her act. So there was a God after all! Jane stood on a small platform on stage and posed in the nude except for small strips of silk. I had to lie on my back behind the platform and watch Jane pose. Each time the curtain closed I'd take the silk piece from her and hand her another piece. Laying there on those hard boards I remember thinking – what a job, what a view!"*

From the perspective of the audience though, Jane appeared framed in one of four frames or boxes, cut out to resemble the frames of a newspaper cartoon strip. Starting in the first box, Jane would pose to represent the opening of the storyline. Back-lit, or bathed in subdued light, Jane would also be behind a translucent screen and as still as a statue. The glamour of the theatre and excitement of modelling Jane, however, was not the full extent of Chrystabel's war work.

Mindful of the ever-watchful eye of the Ministry of Labour, and maybe ENSA, Chrystabel often turned her hand to visiting military hospitals to see injured servicemen, or sometimes giving pep-talks to factory workers. Most bizarre of all her wartime duties was surely her involvement in the

National Fuel Economy Campaign and attending, amongst other related events, the campaign's exhibition at Scunthorpe where she enthusiastically extolled the virtues of coal economy – proclaiming the important part that coal was playing in the war effort! A more unglamorous wartime role for Jane can hardly be imagined. Not surprisingly, Chrystabel apparently did not keep any memorabilia of her coal promotion days! The enthusiastic press coverage though, rather conjures up on image of Miss Tractor Factory of the USSR instead of our svelte English blonde beauty! "*C'est la guerre*", as the French would say.

Away from the coal-face so to speak, each theatre show, in each town, was subject to the scrutiny of the local Watch Committees intent on protecting public morals and upholding the level of decency considered appropriate for the period. Whatever the show's content however, Jane's little-girl-lost voice and coy demeanour cleverly disguised the saucier element of the show. Somehow, even the *double entendre* of certain parts of her act seemed entirely innocent when sung out in her girlie voice, none more so than her famous "Wouldn't you like to be my little dog?" monologue routine. Each show, without fail, included that same ditty – usually to the accompaniment of rapturous applause and stamping of feet. In a sing-song voice it went:

Jane's show always involved Chrystabel getting a serviceman onto stage and singing as she danced with him. Inevitably, it also involved Fritzi running onto the stage and barking furiously at the interloper. Here, she dances with a rather self-conscious soldier.

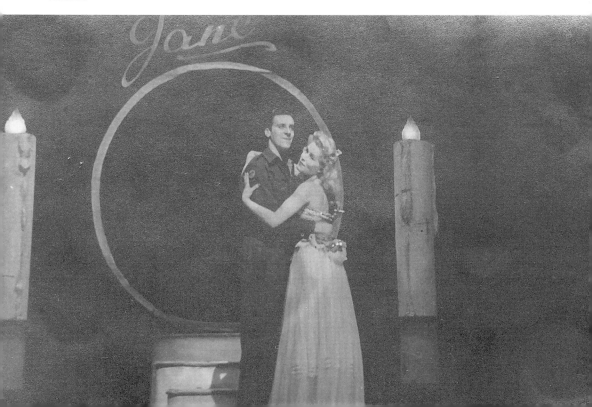

If you read the *Mirror* daily, not of course including Sundays,
You will see how very gaily I display my limbs and undies.
For every day something comes undone, and even though my
    boyfiend is a Copper,
And he sees me through my Blitzes,
Yet – if I should ever come a cropper – his view cannot compare with
    Fritz's!
And my little dog laughed to see such fun!

In the *Daily Mirror* cartoons, I'm sometimes on the rings,
Watched, of course, by Fritz my little dog.
And the clever man who draws me, makes me say such witty things,
Not understood by any kind of dog.
I'm sometimes at my wits' end, and the boys get thrilled to bits.
Drawings show my "end" quite often, and they sometimes show
    my ... bits!
But even when I'm upside down its nothing new to Fritz.
Wouldn't you like to be my little dog?

Not to Georgie, or to any other boy, can I say all I feel
Except, of course, to Fritz my little dog.
Sometimes I'm OK, you know, but sometimes I'm a heel
But always I'm a darling to my little dog.
When Fritz and I are quite alone, then everything is swell.
I cuddle him and whisper things, and all the truth I tell.
I tell him all my nicest thoughts, and naughty ones as well!
Wouldn't you like to be my little dog?

Fritz is very, very clean, a lovely sort of fawn,
He doesn't smell like any other dog,
As a matter of fact – I always use Du Barrys Golden Morn,
When once a month I bath my little dog.
I soap him all over, then rinse him with a hose,
He runs around and shakes himself – like all dogs do I s'pose.
I undress before I bath him, or he'd ruin all my clothes.
Wouldn't you like to be my little dog?

Fritz is just a Dachsund, and he's only ankle high.
Yet lots of boys are jealous of my little dog.
Ankle high is good enough, they say and wink an eye.
Oh Jane, they cry, we'd love to be your little dog.
Fritz sees everything there is – he's like a little elf.
He sees me when I'm stretching to get things off a shelf.
In fact, he sees a lot of things I've hardly seen myself.
Wouldn't you like to be my little dog?

I think you'd better write me a letter.
Just to tell me … wouldn't you like to be my little dog?

Family friends Cliff and Jill White recall Chrystabel singing this little song for the last time at a Millenium New Year's Eve party, and not very long before she died, in her home town of Horsham. Singing it under the stars, word-perfect, Cliff recalled: " *I think that we all knew, and Jane* (sic) *did, that this was likely to be her last New Years Eve. I certainly did. It was a lovely but very poignant moment and, really, Jane's last performance ever.*"

As Chrystabel later admitted, "My Little Dog" was an incredibly silly routine although it always went down well with the audiences. So well, in fact, that one of her production companies even had a 78-RPM record cut of Jane singing the song. *"Thankfully, it never went on general release"*, said Chrystabel, quipping: *"I don't think the world was ready for Jane the singer!"* Twelve-year-old George Dugdale – one of her many young fans – managed to sneak into a matinée of Jane's performance at the Grand Theatre, Southampton, and recalled the reaction to the routine from a number of sailors in the audience. *"I felt embarrassed because the seamen from one of the docked ships, who had seats in the Gods, whistled and threw down money onto the stage."* And that was just the reaction from the audience to one of the fully-clothed numbers, so it is not hard to see why Sheila Davidson was astounded by the audience reaction to the more risqué elements of Jane's show at the Boscombe Hippodrome. *"I was only ten or eleven, and I was amazed to see the nude figure of Jane behind a see-through curtain in various poses. Most of the time we couldn't see a thing as the Yanks were all on their feet, shouting and whistling, and blocking our view."*

Cliff White, recalling a Jane stage show at the Palace Theatre, Grimsby, told how seemingly prim and proper workmates, who would never so much as dream of buying *Health & Efficiency* magazine, made sure they had front-row seats for the performance – one even smuggling in a camera!

All around the country, and often risking bombs and bullets, Chrystabel continued to put on her show to great and growing public acclaim. Despite all the jollity and fun of the Jane stage shows however, the dangerous reality of the war was never far away. Ever present in Chrystabel's mind was the overbearing worry of Arthur's safety. For Chrystabel herself, as for every man, woman and child in the British Isles, the ever-present threat of air attack loomed, although it was certainly always a case of "the show must go on" when it came to her stage performances. During the July and August of 1942, Chrystabel was playing The Empire in Bristol and it was while she was here that the city suffered its worst single bombing incident of the war in an

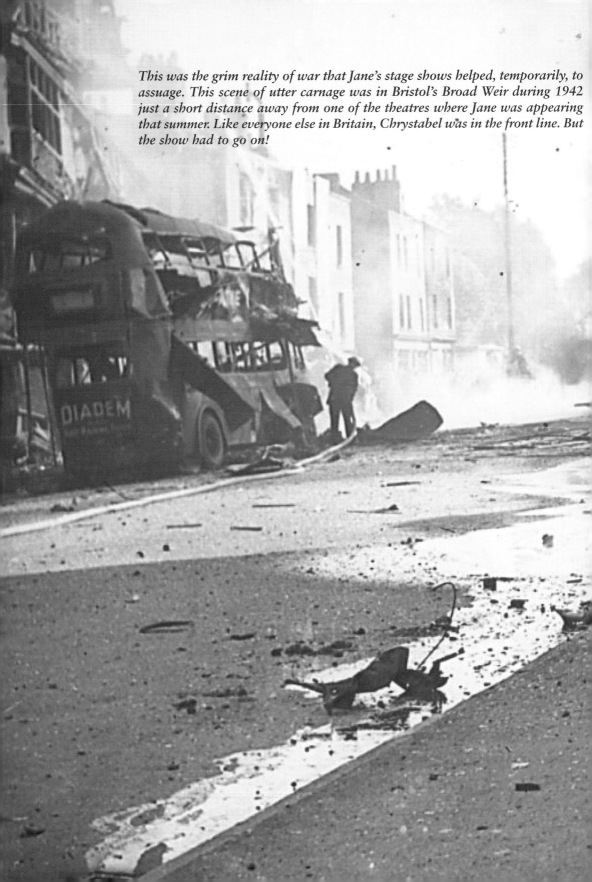

This was the grim reality of war that Jane's stage shows helped, temporarily, to assuage. This scene of utter carnage was in Bristol's Broad Weir during 1942 just a short distance away from one of the theatres where Jane was appearing that summer. Like everyone else in Britain, Chrystabel was in the front line. But the show had to go on!

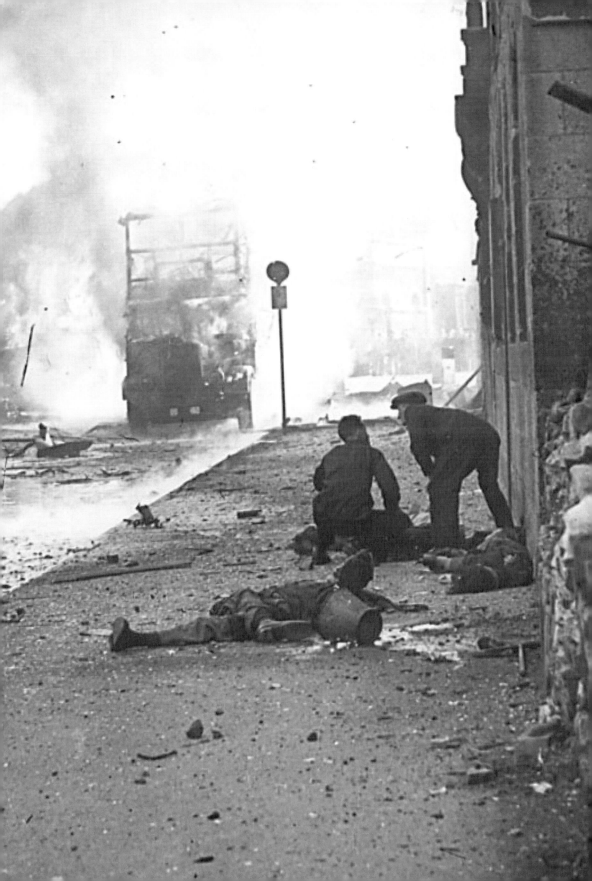

event that was to traumatise the community. On 28 August 1942, a solitary Luftwaffe Junkers Ju 86R high-altitude bomber released a single 250kg bomb from an altitude of seven miles, sending it down to fall in Broad Weir just a short distance from the theatre. Carnage was caused in the crowded street as the bomb detonated, killing forty-eight people, seriously injuring twenty-six and with another thirty slightly hurt. Like everyone else in the country, Chrystabel was in the front line. Hull and Grimsby during 1943 were both on Chrystabel's itinerary and the German air force were again on her tail with heavy raids – most particularly in Grimsby where anti-personnel or Butterfly bombs caused widespread alarm and disruption. But still the show went on!

In the theatre foyers wherever she appeared, glass-fronted display panels showing promotional pictures of Jane were regularly smashed by fans eager to obtain souvenirs. Often, the stolen photographs were later thrust in front of Chrystabel for autographing. Once, at Croydon, there was such a crush to see Jane by autograph hunters and followers that Chrystabel had to be protected by mounted Police officers. Such was the price of her fame – a timelessly prevalent trend when it comes to fans in pursuit of their idols; witness the mobbing of pop stars and footballers in the twenty-first century. Some things never change!

Usually, as part of a variety act, Chrystabel would often be billed as Britain's Perfect Girl, sometimes as Jane out of the *Daily Mirror* – or else Just Jane. Interestingly, and as the war progressed, so Pett and Freeman pushed yet further the boundaries of acceptability with both storyline and artwork – a trend that was mirrored in the stage acts. Continuing well past the end of the war and into the late 1940s and early 1950s, the shows were billed finally as what they became – striptease acts. Defensively, Chrystabel remained insistent that even these later shows were both artistic and respectable. She was horrified by the prospect of being seen as just a stripper rather than an artiste. James Carroll, an East Ham Air Raid Warden agreed. *"I went to see her show several times at the East Ham Palace. Yes – the performance was naughty for the period, but somehow very respectable at the same time. I know that seems a bit of a contradiction in terms but it's difficult to put a finger on it really. You couldn't take offence though."*

Taking a similar view was Sidney White, resident percussionist with the house orchestra at Bristol's Empire Theatre who recalled Jane as "... a comparatively respectable nude." She was not, it appears, in the same league as the great Phyllis Dixey of the same period and who billed herself as a fan dancer. In reality, Dixey was, as described elsewhere, "a tasteful nude artiste", although others less kind might have just called her a stripper! Whatever, her act was a nude one going by the name of "Peek-a-boo" and she herself was often billed as "The Girl the Lord

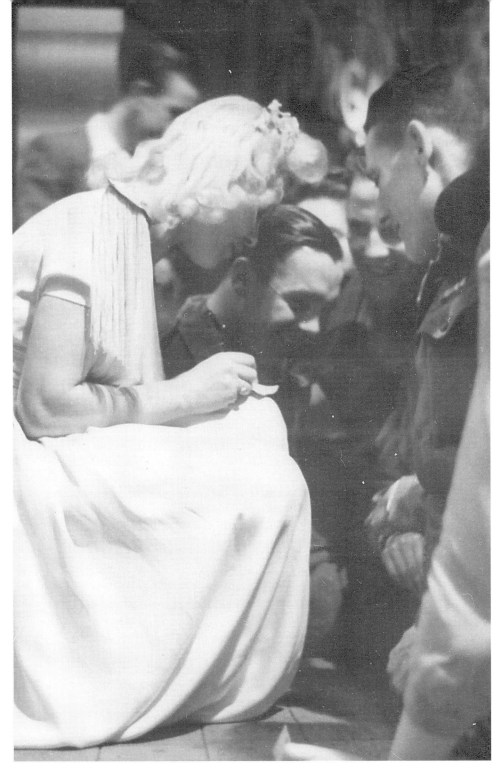

After each stage show, fans clamoured for Jane autographs from the star of the show. Here, she obliges servicemen from an appreciative audience during a wartime performance. Front of house publicity photos were often stolen so that they could be autographed by the Daily Mirror *heroine!*

Chamberlain Banned" – a dubious accolade never quite afforded Jane. That said, it had often been a close-run thing.

There were, of course, those who *did* take offence at Jane and towards the end of her career Chrystabel had been signed by Lew and Leslie Grade. *"One night"*, recalled Chystabel, *"I had just done my strip routine and I spotted two Policemen standing at the back of the auditorium. I thought to myself – that's it, my career is finished, the Grades are ruined – I'm done for. Then, after the show, the two Policemen came to my Dressing Room. I knew that I was obviously about to be arrested. "Evenin' miss. We've just come to tell you the magistrates 'ave decided your little dog don't need no performing licence after all. Thank you miss! Good night." Well, I've never been so relieved in all my life! When the curtains closed that night I really had thought that for me it was curtains for good."*

Had it been curtains for good, then there would certainly have been an outcry amongst the troops, and although not part of the official troop-entertaining ENSA organisation, she did a number of morale-boosting appearances for "her" boys in April and May of 1944 and during the immediate run-up to the D-Day landings. Chrystabel had vivid memories of those events:

"By the end of May 1944 it was clear that the invasion of the continent was imminent. I was in theatre at Bournemouth and there were troops everywhere. There were even tanks in the cul-de-sac where our theatrical lodging house was situated and with soldiers waterproofing their vehicles.

"One day the manager of the theatre in Bournemouth called me into his office. When I got there I was told the Army wanted me to go and entertain some troops in the New Forest. They had been due to land in France but had been unable to sail due to bad weather and so were getting very bored and restless.

"I was put into a car with curtains all around the passenger windows so I could not see where I was going and then driven off to an unknown destination. Next, I found myself in a huge military encampment. There were tents and marquees, lorries and equipment for as far as you could see – and thousands upon thousands of soldiers sitting around looking so absolutely bored.

"When the soldiers saw me I was given a marvellous welcome. I gave a little speech wishing them luck, sung them a few silly songs and got one or two of the boys up on stage with me. I remember signing good luck messages on bits of kit – lifejackets, tents, cigarette packs – all those sorts of things, and, of course, copies of the Daily Mirror. *I wonder if any of them survive today? Anyway, the sense of tension was almost touchable and yet so very unbearable, but I think I helped ease the anxiety just a little bit.*

"The next day I was asked to entertain more troops and was again driven off with curtains over the windows. We arrived at what I now know was Hurn airport near Bournemouth, an RAF base. This time I was entertaining Typhoon pilots of 182 Squadron – of course, that was my husband's squadron. I suppose a string or two had been pulled to get me there! Again, it was an impromptu performance. Amid all the excitement, though, I could not help wondering just how many would be coming back, or even if my Arthur would be safe. But he had a job to do, and so did I. I had to keep a stiff upper lip and all that stuff!

"The next day, backstage, we heard that the invasion had started. There was a lot of excitement, but a lot of worry too. Looking back, these few performances were the most memorable moments in my life – just my little bit in the great D-Day story".

At the height of her popularity during the late war years, Jane also had her imitators. Conscious of the widespread impact that Jane was having upon the majority of men in the armed services, it was only natural that

During a performance at an RAF base, a corporal airman gets rather carried away in his clinch with Jane and causes severe distraction amongst members of the orchestra! Although not a member of the official ENSA, Chrystabel regularly performed for the services at what were deemed to be the rather less boisterous venues.

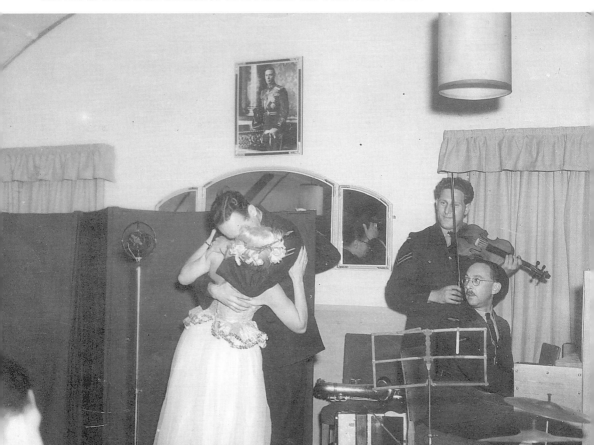

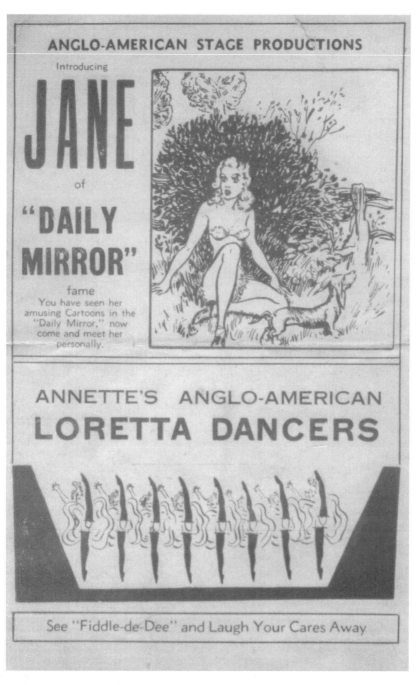

Jane was billed during her stage career as Jane of the Daily Mirror *or, sometimes, Britains Most Perfect Girl which reflected her pre-war triumph as Miss Venus.*

52

THE MODEL FOR "JANE" OF THE
"DAILY MIRROR" CARTOON

BRITAIN'S MOST PERFECT GIRL

Miss Chrystabel Leighton Porter

many young girls of the period would want to copy her style. Consequently, the dresses and hair drawn on Jane by Pett were widely copied by young ladies the length and breadth of Britain, and some even went to the extent of buying themselves a Dachshund dog! "Jane Look-alike" contests grew in popularity, and Chrystabel herself judged one such competition held in The Dome at Brighton when she presented the winner with a voucher for cosmetics – although it is said that the look-alikes generally fled when Chrystabel came to town. As the old saying goes, imitation is always the sincerest form of flattery. Such, then, was the extent of Jane-mania at this period, although it must remain a puzzle as to exactly what it was about a mere cartoon character that sparked such a devoted and, at times, an almost cult-like following.

The partnership with Lew and Leslie Grade continued well on into the post-war years, and seems to have been a lucrative one for all parties. Capitalising on her star status, the Grades often gave Jane top billing and whilst she was clearly the main draw it is not to detract from her stage career to say that, quite often, she would share the billing with accomplished and popular artistes – musicians, dancers and comedians alike. However, it was without doubt Jane who brought in the money and on 12 August 1946, the Grade brothers sent Chrystabel a telegram: "Sincerest congratulations on breaking house record August 5th Aston Hippodrome. Regards Lew and Leslie". For the Grades to have sent this telegram they must have been smiling all the way to the bank. And so was Chrystabel. For a while around 1952, Jane became a solo act, no longer part of variety and sharing the billing – but her very own show. This, in the early post-war years, was the pinnacle of her fame, popularity and success. As ever, it wouldn't last.

By the end of her stage career, and well into the late fifties and even the early sixties, Chrystabel had sometimes shared the billing with some of the big variety names of the time – Max Wall, Morecambe and Wise, Ann Shelton, Elsie and Doris Walters, Stanelli, Frankie Vaughan, Dickie Henderson, Benny Hill, Roy Hudd, Jon Pertwee, Roy Castle and Billy Cotton amongst them. Of these, Benny Hill had once

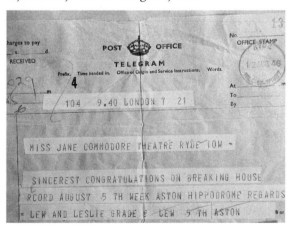

By 1946 Jane was earning an awful lot of money for both Chrystabel and the Grade brothers. Seldom moved to thank or acknowledge their stars for financial success, the week at the Aston Hippodrome must have been exceptional for it to have caused Lew and Leslie to send this congratulatory telegram to Chrystabel.

Jane

There must be many ex servicemen who remember a scene like this as Jane dances with an RAF airman picked from the audience during one of her stage shows against the "Jane" backdrop.

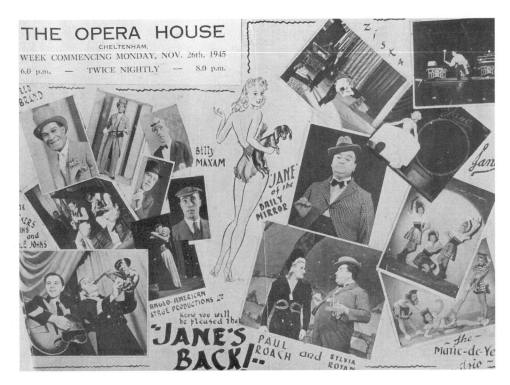

Just after the war's end and the Jane show arrived at The Opera House, Cheltenham, where the programme prominently featured Norman Pett artwork and mentioned the Daily Mirror. *Publication of this image prompted copyright claims from Pett who eventually secured a fee from Anglo-American Productions for its use. Similarly, the* Daily Mirror *wrote tetchily to the producer reminding him of his obligations under copyright laws but took no further action. For their part, Anglo-American and later Lew and Leslie Grade went on exploiting the* Daily Mirror *connection without redress.*

been the Drury family's milkman in Eastleigh and Benny had been smitten, apparently, by the young Chrystabel. When he later met her on stage he was very coy and insufferably shy, she recalled, but in due course she was amused by his "Ernie the Milkman" song and recalled him delivering her daily pinta! Later, much later, Benny would confide to her that memories of Chrystabel as a young girl had inspired him to write a song about his milkman days – a tale he possibly told for effect rather than having any foundation in the truth. As for Roy Hudd, his 1997 book "Cavalcade of Variety Acts" paid further tribute to her stage performances as Jane when she had appeared the length and breadth of the country. To name but very few: The Opera House Cheltenham, Theatre Royal Stockport, The Hippodrome Norwich, The Grand Theatre Brighton, The Empire Theatre York, The Kilburn Empire,

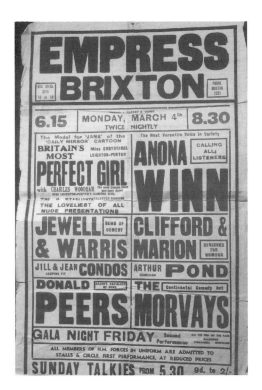

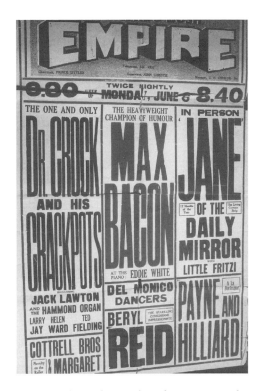

The Empress Theatre at Brixton billed Chrystabel as "Britain's Most Perfect Girl" and made only a secondary reference to her as Jane from the Daily Mirror *– although she shared top billing in this variety show with singer Anona Winn.*

Across the other side of town at The Shepherds Bush Empire, she was billed as "Jane of the Daily Mirror*" and appeared with regular co-stars, the comedian Max Bacon and the unlikely sounding Dr Crock & His Crackpots. Also on the bill were the Del Monico Dancers, with whom Jane frequently toured and appeared. Also on the same bill is the famous Beryl Reid.*

Chelsea Palace Theatre, New Theatre Cardiff, The Tivoli Hull, Theatre Royal Hanley, The Commodore Ryde, The Grand Theatre Southampton, The Davis Theatre Croydon, The Cambridge Theatre, The Blackpool Palace Theatre and the Hackney Empire were amongst some of the many venues graced by Chrystabel's performance of Jane.

Despite the height of Jane's strip cartoon popularity being indisputably over the wartime years, it was the late 1940s and early 1950s that saw the height of her stage popularity, with Jane shows being at their peak. During this time, Chrystabel had negotiated a minimum of 10% of the shows' gross takings, with an additional guaranteed fee for appearing. Surviving receipts show that some weekly takings were in the thousands of pounds bracket, and so minimum fees payable to Chrystabel for these performances would have stood at at least one hundred pounds. This, of course, at a time when average weekly wages were counted in maybe three, four or five pounds. Putting it further into perspective, it was at a time when professional footballers were earning twenty pounds a week. The great Stanley Matthews, drawing huge crowds at football matches every Saturday,

Although taken towards the end of her stage career when she was in her late thirties or even early forties, this is a typical Jane stage pose as Chrystabel cavorts in a grass skirt with a troupe from the Del Monico Dancers.

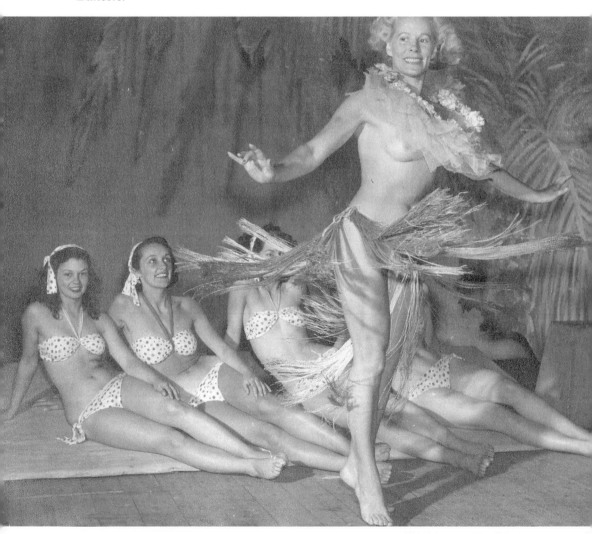

even earned just a mere twenty pounds weekly, but with a generous two pound bonus for a win or a consolation one pound payment for a draw. It was still some time yet before the England Football Captain, Johnny Haynes, became the first hundred pound a week player – but he had long been left behind by the otherwise unknown actress and model who played, and was, Jane.

Whilst the stage shows outlived the strip cartoon it was inevitable that, eventually, the shows would come to a natural end. For one thing, Chrystabel was past her first flush of youth and, whilst still a strikingly good-looking woman, the little girlie performance was hardly credible for much longer. Jane on stage had run its course, was now old hat and on the way to rapidly becoming passé. Radio, though, was a different matter and Chrystabel, taking the part of Jane, appeared in the show Radio Roundup alongside Cardew Robinson during 1951. In a way it was her showbiz swansong.

Keith Riley was at her last stage performance in the Leeds City Varieties Music Hall (popularly known as "The Verts") and recalled the compère's announcement:

At the height of her stage career as Jane during the late 1940s and early 1950s, Chrystabel was earning what might be considered very considerable sums of money for the period. This batch of retained payment advice slips and contracts tell their own story of showbiz success, notable among them being ones from Lew and Leslie Grade.

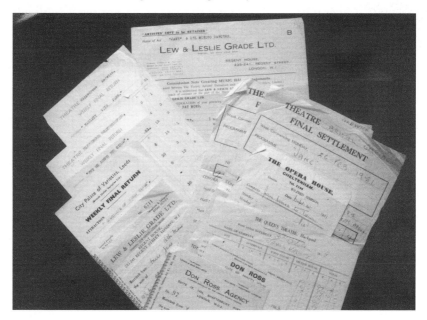

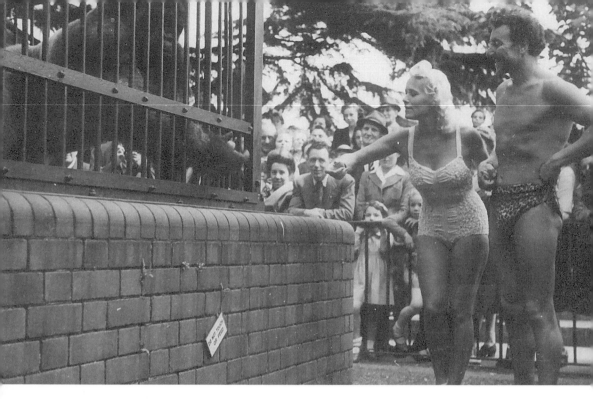

Wherever she went on tour she caused a sensation, and whichever town she starred in she was called upon for other appearances, War Weapons Weeks, Salvage Drives, Dig For Victory and Fuel Economy all being campaigns to which she was enlisted in what Chrystabel called "my extra bit for the war effort." Here, in a rather more fun appearance, she is seen at Bristol's Zoo during its immediate post-war re-opening. Rather predictably, the newspapers could not resist captioning this photo of her with an unidentified circus performer: "Me Tarzan, you Jane."

Finally, after a period of almost demure and coy billing of the Jane act, the posters eventually proclaimed "JANE STRIPS!" at the very end of her career, describing her as the greatest striptease Queen of them all. It was, perhaps, an unfair description of Chrystabel who was certainly not a striptease artiste in the accepted sense. But advertising is advertising, and doubtless the description put bums on seats.

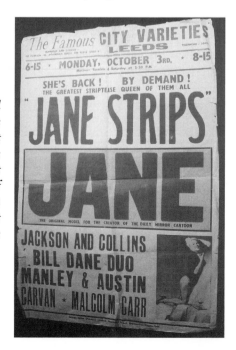

"Ladies and gentlemen, as you know this is sadly Jane's last performance. She has asked me to thank you all for your support, letters and flowers this week. She says this last performance is for her biggest fan, Arthur, who is in the audience tonight". "Lucky Arthur!", muttered someone sitting close by".

Almost as a post-script to her stage career, Chrystabel had at some point developed a professional relationship with Paul Raymond, more recently famous for London's *Raymond Revue Bar*. According to Arthur, this may have been as early as 1947. For a number of years it is believed that Chrystabel had helped select and coach the girls for the later *Revue Bar* shows. Her son Simon, an RAF fighter pilot flying Phantoms in the 1970s and 80s, recalls how the best tickets in the house were almost always available, on tap, for himself and his RAF squadron colleagues to attend the *Raymond Revue Bar*, although Chrystabel herself remained reticent about the extent of her business arrangements with Raymond. Whilst times and attitudes change, the nature of these shows was very far removed indeed from the world of Jane on stage in Hi-Diddle-Diddle! Jane had been almost innocently burlesque by comparison to the far from innocent and raunchy Paul Raymond shows, and it is true to say that had Chrystabel's involvement been generally known about then it is possible that she may have feared tarnishing an almost squeaky-clean Jane image. Again, she surely did not want to let her old fans down.

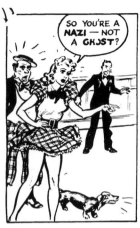

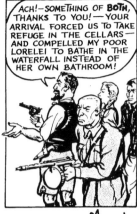

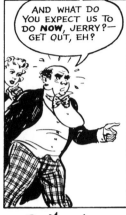

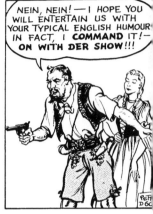

Monday. 12 March.

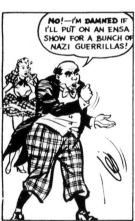

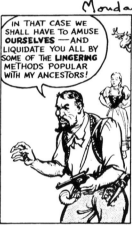

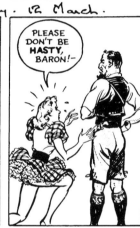

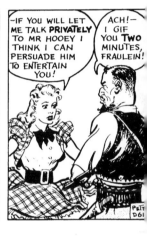

Tuesday. 13 March.

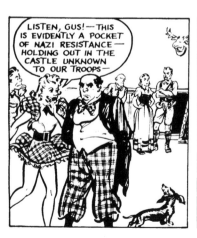

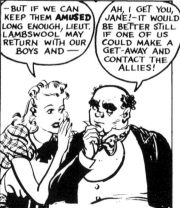

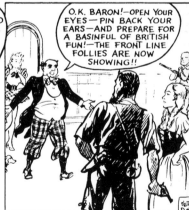

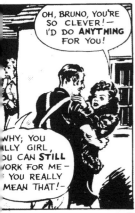

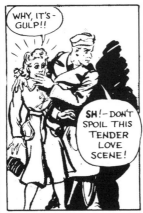

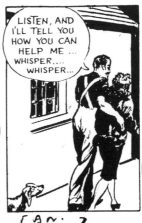

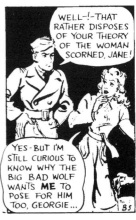

THURSDAY   JAN. 7

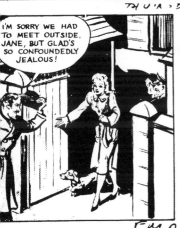

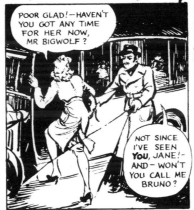

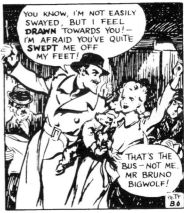

FRIDAY   JAN. 8

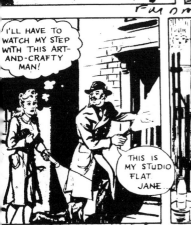

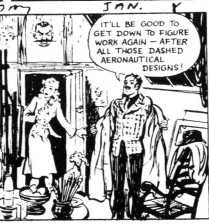

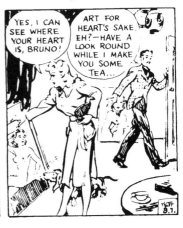

63

Chapter Five

Of Nudes and Prudes

"The book of life", wrote Oscar Wilde, "began with a man and a woman in a garden and ended in Revelations." According to the renowned critic and journalist Hannen Swaffer, so did the story of Jane.

Nudity, or even partial nudity, of just about any description during the nineteen forties, was socially far less acceptable than, say, by the more enlightened nineteen sixties. Indeed, stage nudity was just about unheard of then, and it is true to say that even by the progressive sixties stage nudity in musical shows like "Hair" still caused a furore. But it wasn't just the authorities that the promoters of the Jane stage shows had to contend with, and Chrystabel herself recalls being accosted by two charming elderly ladies who asked if she couldn't think of anything better to do to help the war effort than to take her clothes off. Chrystabel replied that she didn't think so, because she hadn't been trained to do anything else. *"I suppose I was the only person whose war work was getting undressed! I was also about the only person in Britain who didn't mind about the shortage of clothes"*, she later reflected.

The extent of the sensation caused by the "Jane" stage shows, though, during the nineteen forties was nothing short of exceptional, and the controls exerted by the authorities could be draconian in the extreme. Overall responsibility for regulating what might be deemed to be socially and morally acceptable standards rested with the Lord Chamberlain's Office, although thereafter there were always the local Public Watch Committees to satisfy. These arbiters of public decency could, at a whim, pull the plug, locally, on any performances that they considered to be inappropriate, and did so without recourse to appeal and without any need to justify their actions. Not infrequently did they do just that for the Jane stage performances, and were it not for the meddlings of the various elected members then the list of towns played by Jane would have been that much longer. Notable in causing difficulties, the Watch Committees of Norwich and Waltham Green were no particular fans of Jane, but it was the Lord Chamberlain's Office whom Chrystabel feared the most. At a stroke they could have her shows closed down and banned on a nationwide basis. *"The Watch Committees"*, she recalled, *"would often make a fuss about this or that, and have some stipulation about how aspects of the show should*

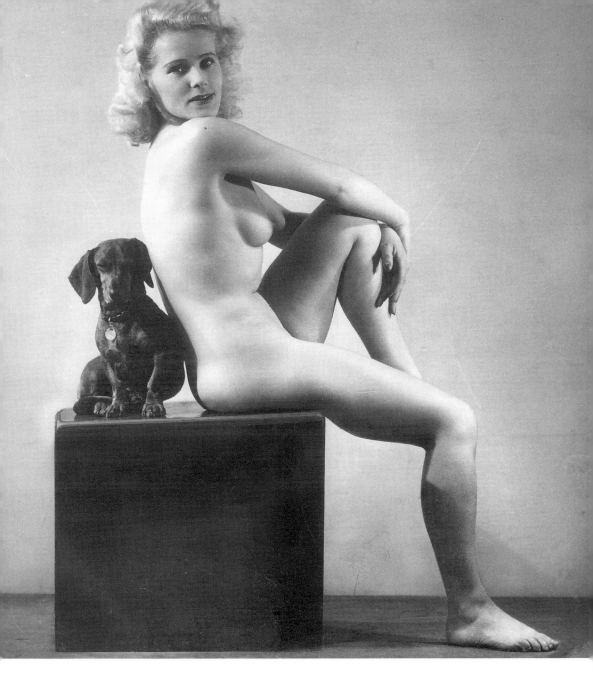

Stage nudity was somewhat uncommon and certainly very strictly controlled during
the nineteen forties. Each pose had to be modelled in a fixed statuesque stance, with
all movement banned. Once, when the curtains jammed, Chrystabel moved to close
them and caused an absolute sensation in the theatre. Quite likely it was the first
time a nude artiste had ever been seen to move on a British stage.

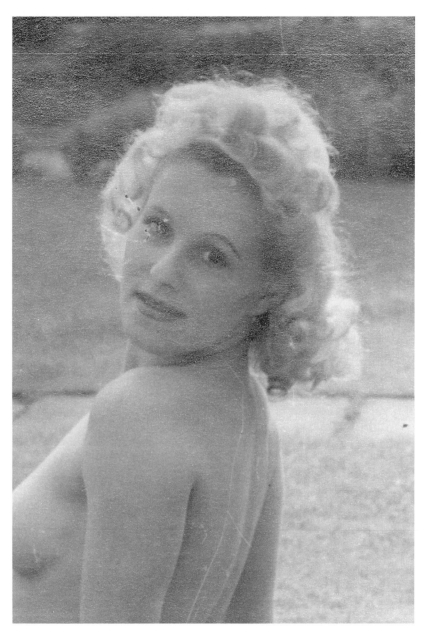

Although the majority of Jane cartoon figures were clothed or semi-clothed, all were drawn from nude poses. Here, Pett works on a Jane pose with Chrystabel at around the time of D-Day in 1944. In the Daily Mirror *of 7 June 1944, D + 1, Jane appeared naked for the first time, sending ripples of excited sensation across all service ranks. Even the nude drawings caused a stir and so it is easy to see the furore that sometimes accompanied stage nudity.*

66

be presented. Sometimes they just banned us from a particular town and that was that. For instance though, one town had a problem with navels of all things and these had to be covered with sticking plaster – and yet breasts or nipples were perfectly fine with them! However, I wouldn't go so far as to say that the committee members were actually bought, although I do know that complimentary tickets were very generously dished out to certain influential members on committees where we knew we had a problem. Even in the few towns that banned us, I recall that the committee members – all men, of course – insisted on sitting through a full performance in order to make sure about their decisions! I well remember the aftermath of one of the towns that rejected the show following the usual preview show, when I later saw the entire pin-stripe-suited committee, and a clutch of attendant portly local government officers, sitting through my performance in the theatre of a neighbouring town! I clearly remember thinking to myself how hypocritical they were, and wondering if their wives knew where they were."

In another town, Chrystabel was instructed to cover her nipples on stage and had the idea of covering them with suitably tasselled silver stars made out of cardboard. The question was, how should she fix the stars to her ample anatomy? Hitting upon an idea, Chrystabel made her way to Halfords car and cycle store and purchased a tube of rubber solution used for fixing bicycle tyre punctures. At first, the idea worked but a little way into the show and disaster struck. The combination of her body heat and the hot stage lighting melted the rubber and in mid-performance the two stars descended gracefully to the stage floor on long fronds of rubber solution. Unable to move (regulations prohibited all nude stage movement) Chrystabel stood in statuesque horror as the audience erupted with applause, whistles and foot stomping. Things didn't always go according to plan.

Later, and as she began to accept the nature of her daughter's occupation, Chrystabel persuaded her mother to attend one of the Jane performances in Southampton – her family's home town. *"I was somewhat concerned about what my mother's reaction would be, so I told her not to worry if it looked as if I was in the nude. I told her just a bit of a big white lie and assured her that of course I wouldn't be naked, and that instead I'd be wearing a flesh-coloured body stocking that would make me appear nude. Well, after the show and on the way home I asked her what she had thought of the performance. "Lovely, my dear", she replied. Then, with an unmistakably wicked twinkle in her eye, she said: "… but that body stocking was really looking a bit grubby, Chrys. Shall I take it home and wash it for you?"*

The Lord Chamberlain's office though, could not be fooled by blatant body stocking claims, and it was with considerable trepidation that

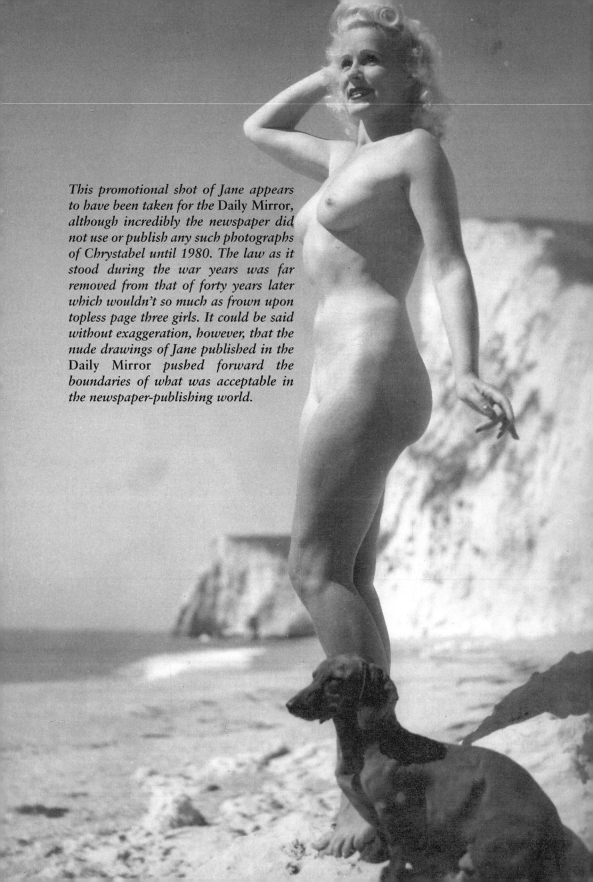

This promotional shot of Jane appears to have been taken for the Daily Mirror, although incredibly the newspaper did not use or publish any such photographs of Chrystabel until 1980. The law as it stood during the war years was far removed from that of forty years later which wouldn't so much as frown upon topless page three girls. It could be said without exaggeration, however, that the nude drawings of Jane published in the Daily Mirror pushed forward the boundaries of what was acceptable in the newspaper-publishing world.

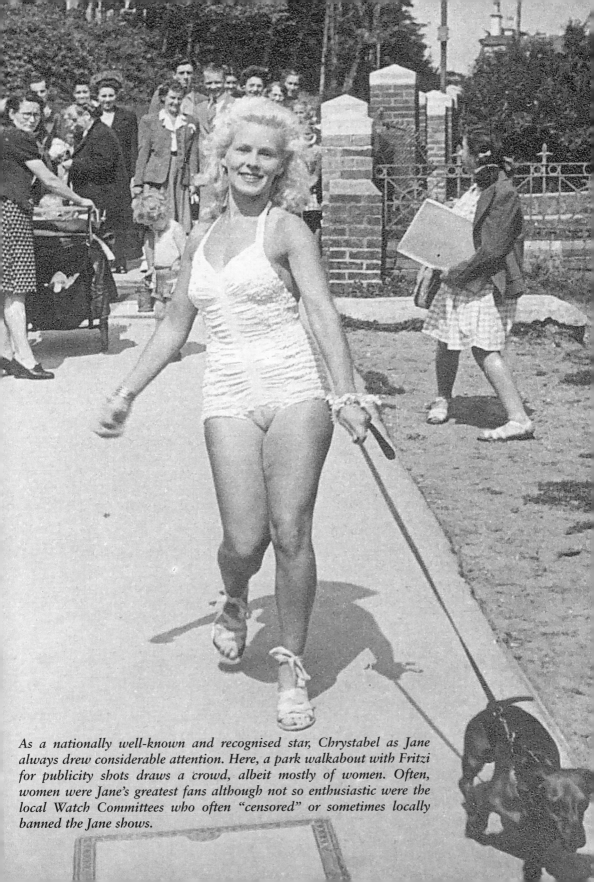

As a nationally well-known and recognised star, Chrystabel as Jane always drew considerable attention. Here, a park walkabout with Fritzi for publicity shots draws a crowd, albeit mostly of women. Often, women were Jane's greatest fans although not so enthusiastic were the local Watch Committees who often "censored" or sometimes locally banned the Jane shows.

Chrystabel was once called before an official there to explain her act. *"I understand you pose naked"*, said the Civil Servant, *"... but what about your breasts? How do you cover them?"* Thinking quickly, Chrystabel responded: *"Well sir, I cover them with my hands"*. The reality, of course, was that she didn't! Astonished, the official could only splutter *"Goodness me! You must have jolly big hands!"* But it was not just those in Watch Committees and government offices who would have their say about Jane, and even the strip cartoon would have its detractors and critics. Letters to the *Daily Mirror* of the "Disgusted of Tunbridge Wells" type were far from infrequent, although rarely ever published.

Typical was one such letter from a correspondent simply calling himself "Let's Be Decent." It was one of the few that saw the light of day.

> *"Sir: I am truly disgusted with the absurd letters which have appeared from time to time concerning Jane.*
>
> *"Would "Long live Jane" please give me the connection between English war brides and this comic strip, Jane. Really, I fail to grasp that point. If you mean that Jane is the model for these new English war brides then they had better stay where they belong.*
>
> *"Personally, I don't think you know the difference between comedy and drama, as up until now I have not seen anything extra funny in this strip. I have been talking about it with the girls in our office and the verdict was universal – corny. For all it is doing is lowering the high standards of womanhood. I observed also that every letter sent in was from the opposite sex. Well, "Broad Minded", you are definitely right when you call yourself a wolf. I think I know just what type you are when you compare Jane to nature. Don't be so insulting to nature! If enjoying Jane in the nude you might say is your idea of being broad minded, then move along old fella; I think I would rather be narrow-minded.*
>
> *"If you insist that you enjoy Jane so much I would suggest that you have it printed in* Men Only *or* Esquire *or some such other magazine – then you can have your fill and the younger generation wouldn't have to face such immodesty."*

Such immodesty, though, even sparked letters to the press on the other side of the Atlantic with "Respectable Harold" jumping to defend Jane's honour and reputation when writing to the *Toronto Star*. In the case of the *Daily Mirror* letters, Pett later suggested they were phoney and just set up to provoke a reaction. Which, of course, they did, whatever the truth of their origin! "Respectable Harold" in Toronto rose to such provocation:

"Dear Sir: In reply to "Respectable Betty" and Harold Wellwood Jr, I would like to defend the right of free press and freedom for which this war was fought by replying to the condemnation of the comic strip, Jane, that these two individuals have resorted to.

"There is one thing as always that is quite evident when you hear narrow minded selfish people such as these. They have never been near a uniform. The lads who were overseas have more right than anyone else to decide who and what they like. It isn't up to people like these two to make decisions for them. They want Jane, and by popular request it has been syndicated by many papers throughout Canada and the United Stores of America.

"It is easy to see why this does not appear understandable in many ways to Wellwood and "Respectable Betty", because they probably never knew what the war was about or even what went on in the world outside of their own backyards.

"In England, Jane was the biggest hit and part of the daily routine of every serviceman over there. They saw fit to read Jane. They liked Jane. They appreciated Jane. And when they got back to this country they were disappointed because of people like Wellwood and Betty who weren't unselfish enough to make a few sacrifices.

"Well, maybe one of these days someone will teach you that there were men who fought and died for your freedom, and now you want to snatch away something that they want.

"Betty's reference to "your sailor friends" makes a point that sounds to me as if being a sailor is to lower one's dignity. Well, a sailor is one of our Canadian fighting men and he won the war for you and for your zombie friends. Why, I don't know, because he certainly isn't getting much thanks for his efforts from people like you.

"Unfortunately, there is no law in these parts to prevent slander against servicemen by some home-front cookie. There isn't any such law because these same "sailor friends" fought to keep freedom and democracy alive ... if they hadn't, then you wouldn't even be able to make a comment about Jane.

"As has already been pointed out, the comic section is not meant to be a great literary feature of the newspaper. You don't have to read it and there is always Mickey-Mouse, or why not try a crossword puzzle and exercise those feeble brains of yours!

"Signed: Respectable Harold"

Such were the various passions aroused by Jane. On the whole though, the published comments were overwhelmingly supportive although journalist Margot Bennett made a curious study of statistics about the Jane strip cartoon, stating without comment that Jane *"... shows her legs to a distance of at least nine inches above the knee 83 times. She dresses, undresses or is undressed forcibly to reveal the brassiere 14 times, the panties 13 times and both brassiere and pants 51 times. She is also shown full-length behind some inadequate substance such as steam, a nightgown, bathing costume or towel in 24 pictures. She has her clothes blown off by a bomb in 4, takes a bath in 5, falls by parachute in 9 and sits up in bed in 5. She has a double who is shown twice bathing, 6 times in brassiere and pants. There is also a girl called Gladys, who is shown wholly in underwear 13 times and sectionally 3 times. This makes an astonishing total of 232 exposures, partial or complete, in 260 issues of the* Daily Mirror.*"*

Quite what the point was of Bennett's factual observation remains unclear, unless it was to shock the reader as to the scale of Jane's sartorial inelegance. It was made with neither comment nor complaint, and with no inflexion or intonation in the style from which conclusions might be drawn. Not complaining, though, were the troops ashore in Normandy when, on D + 1, Jane finally appeared in the nude. The effect on morale was electrifying. Allegedly, it also impacted upon the course of the war. Remember: this was 1944. Pett's drawings were the nearest equivalent thing to todays page-three girls at this particular period in time.

Looking back, it remains important to understand the moral standards of the time and to appreciate the extent to which Pett's drawings were, indeed, epoch making. An insight into what was generally acceptable and what was not can be drawn from the *Daily Mirror* itself of February 1943. In it, the newspaper strongly makes the case for openness in a widespread campaign to educate the public and servicemen alike on the dangers of Venereal Disease. A sensitive subject in any case, the *Daily Mirror* succeeded in making its case and, largely through the newspaper's efforts, advertising was subsequently allowed that spoke openly about sex organs, intercourse and clap. Words like these were, publicly, wholly taboo – even when it came to health education issues that were every bit as important as public information on air raids and gas attacks. If mere words were unacceptable, even in these scenarios, the sensitivity of images needs no further explanation. A snarling attack on the newspaper's stance came from other quarters in the press, one correspondent exclaiming: *"Is it not any wonder that the* Daily Mirror, *promoters of Jane of the loose morals, should take this stance? This is a moral problem with a medical aspect, not a medical problem with a moral aspect."* It was a little unfair to accuse Jane of being loose, and certainly unkind to link her name to this delicate matter but it is indicative of the strong feelings induced over certain aspects of morality and decency. In this case it is interesting that the *Daily Mirror*, Jane's publisher, should be the champion of the cause – illustrative of that newspaper's place, then, in the forefront of progressive and liberal publishing. Without those attitudes, and the *Daily Mirror*'s willingness to cock a snook at

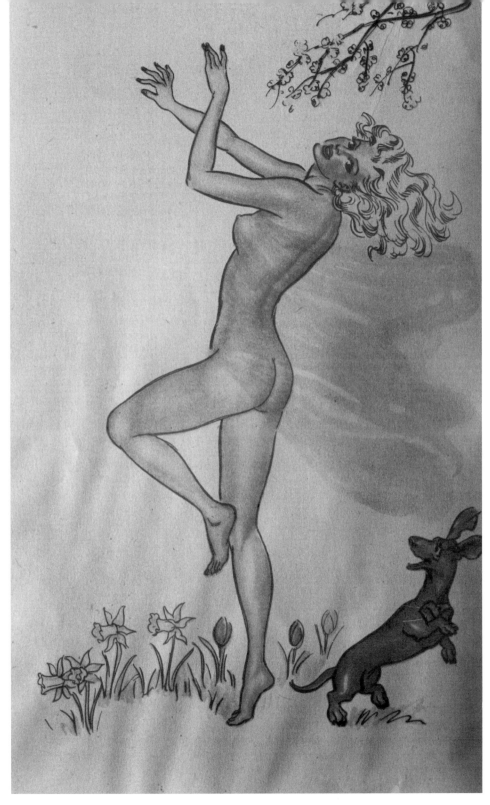

Norman Pett's artistry depicting Jane was extraordinarily prolific with this image probably produced for his Jane's Journal or some other commercial Jane venture.

This informal pose, just pre-war, perhaps gives credence (if ever it were needed!) to Chrystabel's claim that: "If Vera Lynn was the voice of World War Two then Jane was the body!" Little wonder that it was the body that got thousands of troops hot under the collar – and dozens of Watch Committees into a fluster of moral rectitude.

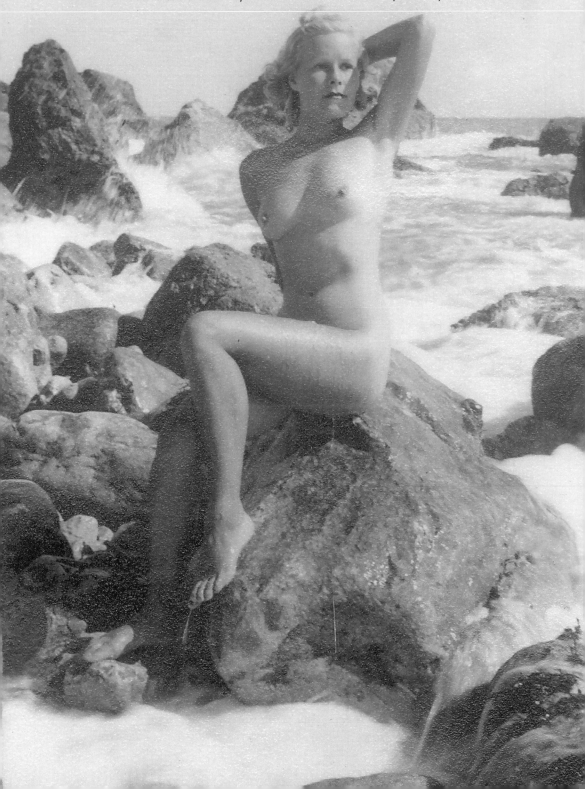

authority and test public moral attitudes, Jane may never have happened in the way that she did.

Commenting in September 1943, Hannen Swaffer wrote of an interview with Pett, when the latter is reported to have said: *"If Jane has to strip for a minor victory, then what shall I have to do with her when we approach Berlin?"* Berlin was almost a year away though, when Jane appeared in the altogether for the very first time. As ever, the storyline was as flimsy as Jane's usual underwear when she was seen on 7th June 1944 taking a bath, behind modesty screens, at an army barracks. Standing up to get a towel that has been left draped over the screens, she knocks them over and is finally exposed in all her glory – after teasing and tantalising her followers throughout four years of war, this was it! At the famed Pegasus Bridge, airborne troops were dropped bundles of the *Daily Mirror* containing these, the latest Jane adventures. Other copies of this edition were soon spread far and wide amongst the invading troops. According to legend, the day these images reached the 36th Infantry Division, the unit advanced some six miles inside German-held territory. The inference in the news stories was that this military achievement was due largely if not entirely to Britain's secret weapon: Jane. In reality, it may certainly have boosted morale and cheered the boys at the front – but sped the advance? Probably not, but it made good copy, nonetheless.

Interestingly, it was not the Lord Chamberlain or the Watch Committees who raised the most serious objection to Jane during her wartime adventures. Instead, it was the Ministry of Information Official Censor who raised concerns about a fairly bizarre security issue. One of Freeman's story lines had Jane involved with a secret aeroplane project, with the craft named the "Meteor X". Visited by two persuasive men in trilby hats and Macintosh coats, and both carrying briefcases marked with the Royal cipher, it was strongly suggested to Pett and Freeman that it might be better for them to name the aircraft "Fighter X", which they agreed to do. Pett later recalled that there was a degree of menace in the suggestion that the name might be changed, although neither man had the faintest idea why the authorities should be so keen to change a seemingly innocent name. That is, not until the RAF's first jet fighter was first unveiled to the public. Its name? Meteor. By chance, Pett had coincidentally stumbled across the then clandestine name of Britain's most secret weapon and had caused some alarm through his coincidental choice of name. Without doubt this was pure coincidence and much along the lines of the scare caused in British Military Intelligence when D-Day code words appeared, coincidentally, in the *Daily Telegraph* crossword. However, living and working at the time in the tiny Gloucestershire village of Toddington, Pett lived not too far from the Gloster aeroplane works at Brockworth. Suspicions were raised. In no time at all, officers of the Special Branch were knocking at

This was the classic Jane pose. In a similar stage pose during her later shows, and when movement restrictions had been partially relaxed, Chrystabel would allow her flimsy attire to fall to the floor and half turn to the audience and it was this act that attracted the attention of the Office of the Lord Chamberlain. Called to his offices to explain the act, she was asked: "How do you cover your breasts?" "Oh, with my hands", she explained. "My word!", exclaimed the official, "you must have very big hands." The Lord Chamberlain, however, never interfered with the Jane acts – unlike her contemporary Phyllis Dixey, who was banned nationally for a time. This Jane poster, devoid of details, was perhaps to have publicised an appearance in one of the towns where the local Watch Committee had said "No".

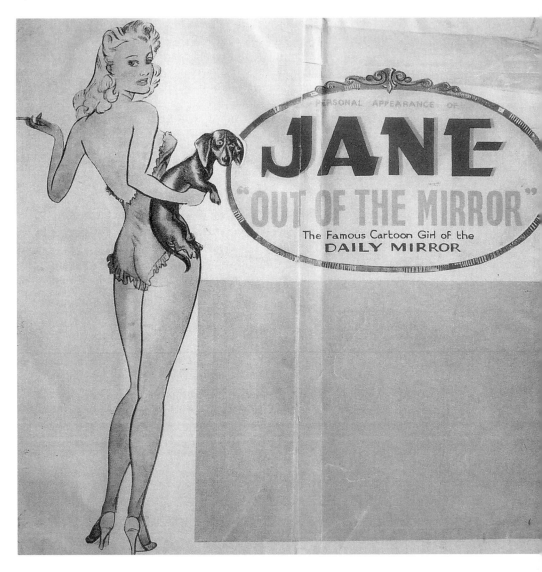

Pett's door but went away satisfied – particularly with the drawing of Jane semi-clad in a Police tunic which he swiftly executed for the Gloucester Police HQ canteen! So Jane, erstwhile secret agent, herself became the centre of a real life security scare. It is quite possible that this little escapade reached the highest levels in Whitehall, and if it did then doubtless it may have brought a wry smile to Churchill's face – although in a few short years he would probably have good cause to rue the existence of Jane. Back to Whitehall though.

According to period magazines that reported on the unusual case, an unnamed Lieutenant Colonel banned the *Daily Mirror* from his men – all panting for Jane – on the basis that, as he put it, Jane was an *"unhealthy sex stimulant"* and it was his duty to *"protect my men from such moral degradation and keep temptation to morality away from them."* Strong words indeed. But the will of his men was stronger. In time, the story of the banned *Daily Mirror* would reach the ears of the newspaper itself. Inevitably, the newspaper ensured that this infringement of the civil liberties of Britain's enlisted men should get to the attention of the War Office in Whitehall and thence on to a sympathetic MP or two. In time, the issue was actually raised in the House of Commons where, it is reported, the Members soberly decided that the officer had overstepped the mark. Rumours persist of references to Jane in Commons debates, although initial scans of Hansard have produced no corroborative proof of this. It seems that this may well be some post-war journalistic embellishment of a ripping good yarn – if ripping is not too unfortunate a descriptive. According to one report though, the armed forces were referred to as "Jane's Fighting Men", probably making a pun on the name of the famous publications "Jane's Fighting Ships" and "Jane's All the World's Aircraft" – named after the publisher rather than our heroine, incidentally! But, if she didn't make any Commons debates, then she certainly made the headlines in at least one Local Government debate. At Wembley, the local rag trumpeted the headline: "*Committee Rejected Plea for Trousers*". The story concerned the weighty issue of the number of pairs of trousers to be provided for the local ambulance service – such was, and is, the gravity of matters debated in Town Hall chambers. Cutting through the pomposity to lighten the interminable debate, Alderman Marshall is reported to have commented on the ambulance mens' threadbare and patched attire – saying that, *"before long they would end up naked, like Jane out of the* Daily Mirror.*"* Wembley Town Hall was not the House of Commons, that is true. But it is a story that shows the universal interest in Jane, not to mention knowledge of her exploits. Later, of course, "Disgusted of Wembley" penned a letter to the newspaper, *"… appalled that such a serious debate should be besmirched by uncalled for references to a smutty tart. What depths of depravity has Alderman Marshall descended to?"*

Strong stuff to say the least. Over the top, certainly. But another illustration that the passions aroused over Jane were not necessarily, or always, confined to the passions of the red-blooded males in the armed services.

Most people loved her. As we have seen, some didn't!

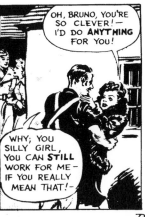

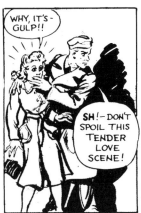

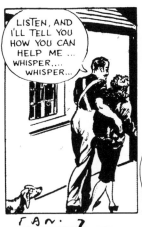

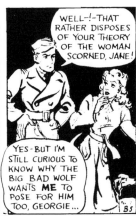

THURSDAY JAN. 7

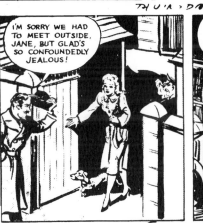

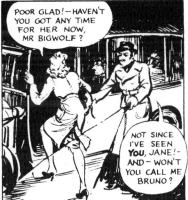

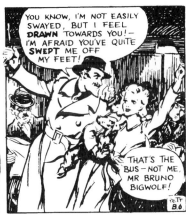

FRIDAY JAN. 8

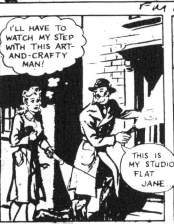

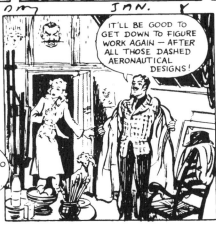

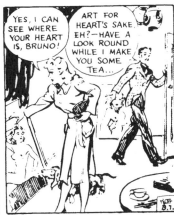

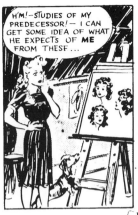

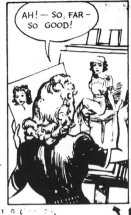

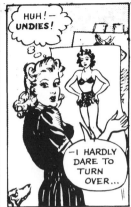

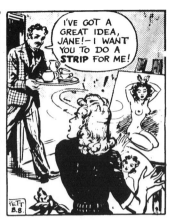

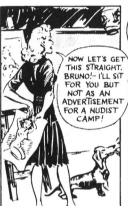

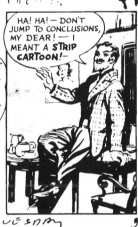

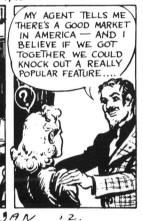

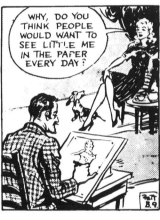

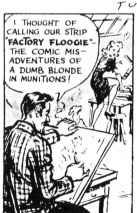

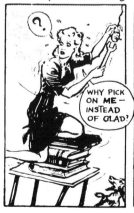

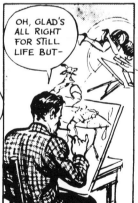

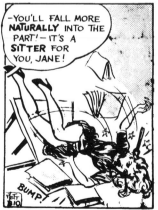

Chapter Six

Of Tanks, Boats and Planes

With her mass appeal to all of the armed services, it was to be expected that Jane's pin-up status would frequently be extended to that of mascot. And so it was. ENSA's G Wilson penned two lines that summed up the sentiments of servicemen everywhere who turned to girls like Jane to brighten and lighten their war when, in description of the pin-up, he succinctly wrote:

> *Cheering the boys who are winning the war,*
> *That's what Pin-Up girls are for!*

Examples abound of Jane's shapely figure appearing on RAF aircraft and on military vehicles, and although Naval discipline precluded her appearance on Naval vessels in the same manner, there were plentiful examples of her form to be found in just about every wardroom and messdeck. The Fleet Air Arm, though, was a different matter, and one of the Fairey Swordfish aeroplanes of number 835 Squadron aboard HMS *Nairana* carried a full-length painting of Jane on her engine cowling. Doubtless, there were other Fleet Air Arm renditions of Jane in what has since become known as nose-art.

Predominantly, it would seem that Jane nose-art figured more on aircraft of RAF Bomber Command than anywhere else, and there are a number of recorded examples. That is not to say that fighter aircraft of RAF Fighter Command did not "become" Jane, although none have surfaced during the research for this book. With Chrystabel Leighton-Porter's husband, Arthur, an RAF fighter pilot on Hawker Typhoons who flew operationally on D-Day, it might well be expected that if any fighter aircraft were to be called after Jane then it would be his. Surprisingly, that wasn't the case. Asked about it in recent years, Arthur remarked:

> *"I don't think it ever occurred to me. There were certainly quite a few examples of artwork on our squadron's Typhoons I think, but it would really have been infra-dig for me to emblazon mine with Jane, wouldn't it? In any case, personalised artwork was not my sort of thing, really."*

So, there we have it – although it would certainly have been nice to present Arthur's Typhoon in this work as depicting our Jane on the cowling! As

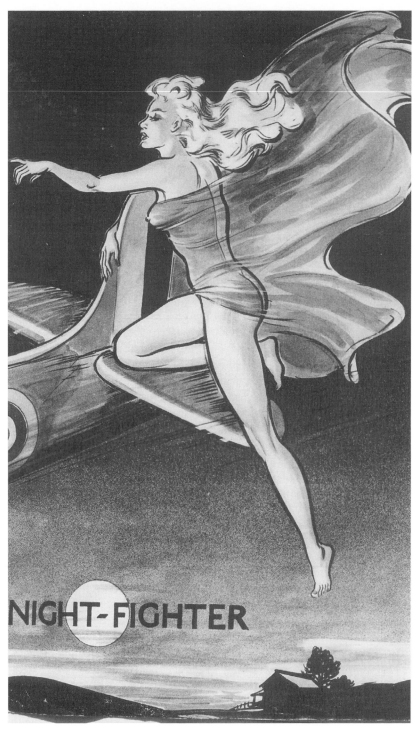

Jane as a pin-up and mascot for the armed forces raised both pulses and morale. Here, this striking Pett artwork was said to have been done originally for an RAF night fighter squadron, although it appeared in a later edition of Jane's Journal.

82

we have seen, however, there was no shortage of other cowlings and fuselages thus decorated, with Avro Lancasters not being an uncommon "canvas" for the multitude of Pett imitators in the Royal Air Force.

Writing to a national newspaper in 1946, a former RAF aircrew member who described himself simply, and rather anonymously, as an "*RAF Navigator from Thame, Oxfordshire*", told a Jane story:

> "*I was interested in your article on Jane of the* Daily Mirror *and heartily agree that she did a great deal for the morale of the RAF. When I was a member of a heavy bomber squadron we had a Lancaster J-Jane with a magnificent life-size picture of Jane painted on the fuselage. The squadron call sign at that time appropriately enough was "Shameless", and "Shameless Jane" as the bomber soon became known was so popular with Flying Control that whenever she called up after a trip she used to traditionally be given top priority to land back at base first.*
>
> "*One night, after a rather "shaky do" with a German fighter, "Shameless Jane" struggled home and made an emergency landing on the Norfolk coast. Some labourers working nearby rushed over to inspect the damage, and after gaping at the holes for some minutes one of them came up to me and said: "The so-and-so certainly made a mess of your kite, but they didn't even manage to get one single hole into Jane. That's why you got home." I couldn't have agreed more wholeheartedly, as anything that had gone through Jane would have hit the pilot. Jane had been his bodyguard that night and she got the whole crew home. Incidentally, the German night fighter was later confirmed as shot down by Jane's gunners and our aircraft went on to do more than seventy trips before being finally shot down and lost.*"

A possible candidate for this RAF Navigator's otherwise unidentified Lancaster could have been "Jane On The Job", a Dunholme Lodge-based Lancaster, although there were certainly others. For example, "Just Jane" of 61 Squadron that went on to achieve an impressive tally of one hundred and twenty-three operational sorties. Although that aeroplane, the original "Just Jane", was Lancaster JB138, she ended her days as an instructional airframe with the RAF's No. 4 School of Technical Training. In reality, "Just Jane" still lives on in the guise of preserved Lancaster NX611 at the East Kirkby, Lincolnshire Aviation Heritage Centre. Here, farmers Fred and Harold Panton have lovingly preserved this Lancaster as a living memorial to their brother Christopher, killed in action while serving as a Navigator with 433 Squadron, Royal Canadian Air Force. It also serves as a tangible reminder of the part Jane played in wartime Britain, NX611 having been restored to represent "Just Jane". For Fred Panton there were additional reasons to name his Lancaster after Jane. Having seen

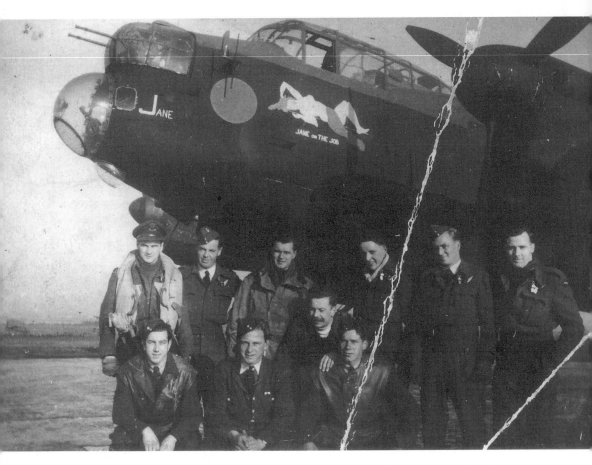

This Lancaster of 170 Squadron at RAF Dunholme Lodge is pictured with its crew in September 1944. In the main, Bomber Command aircraft seem to have been in the majority when it came to replicating the Daily Mirror's Jane. That said, this particular Jane bears only scant resemblance to Pett's creation – but the thought was there!

Chrystabel's Jane at Skegness and fallen in love with her there he later named his daughter after his idol. This Jane, Jane Panton, was not the only baby girl though of the forties and fifties named after the most famous of all cartoon heroines – the name becoming increasingly popular at the height of Jane's fame.

There have been other post-war imitators of the Jane Lancasters, too, with Matchbox model kits producing a 1/72nd scale plastic Lancaster model depicting "Just Jane" and, later on, Corgi die-cast models producing a 1/144th representation of the same aeroplane – both of which delighted Chrystabel. She was equally delighted, too, to visit East Kirkby in 1995 along with a Fritzi look-alike in order to christen "her"

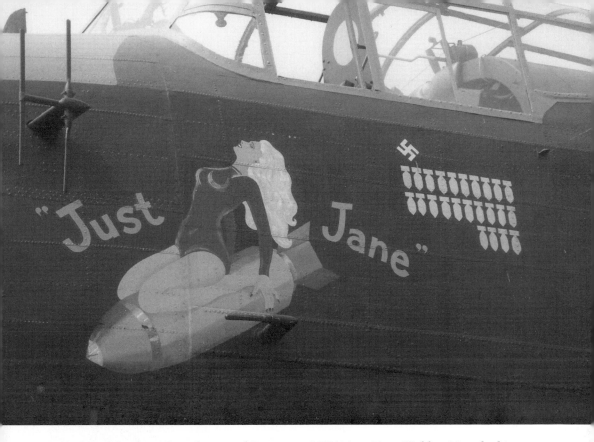

"Just Jane" in the guise of restored Lancaster NX611 at East Kirkby, Lincolnshire, which was visited by Chrystabel Leighton-Porter after completion. The artwork style is typical of the wartime period.

Lancaster. Although not a flying example, "Just Jane" is fully restored to taxiing condition and now has four completely serviceable Rolls-Royce Merlin engines.

In the following chapter, a Vickers Wellington bomber named after Jane is also described. This aeroplane, shot down at Leenstertillen, Holland on 21 June 1942 during a raid to Emden, was Wellington III, X3713, J – Jane of 9 Squadron, RAF, and was in fact the machine flown by the Squadron's Commanding Officer, Wing Commander Leslie James DFC. Predictably, James' Wellington became known on 9 Squadron as "James' Jane" and the loss of the CO, his crew and their flagship bomber was a shattering blow to squadron morale. James, just twenty-five years old, had only been Officer Commanding for a very short while before his death. He and his crew now lie buried in Leens General Cemetery, De Marne, Holland. Chrystabel, on reading their sad story not long before she died, wiped an emotional tear calling them *"All my boys."* And so they were.

Not long after the loss of James and his J-Jane, the squadron re-equipped with Lancasters, but superstition prevented a new Lancaster

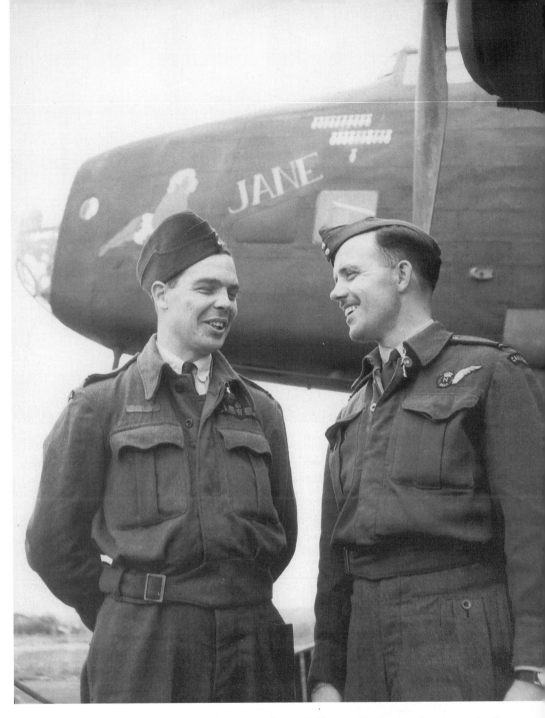

Flying Officer K.A. McCaskill (pilot) and Flying Officer W.J. Coates (navigator) of 427 Squadron Royal Canadian Air Force pictured with their Halifax, "Jane", sporting symbols denoting twenty-one bombing raids.

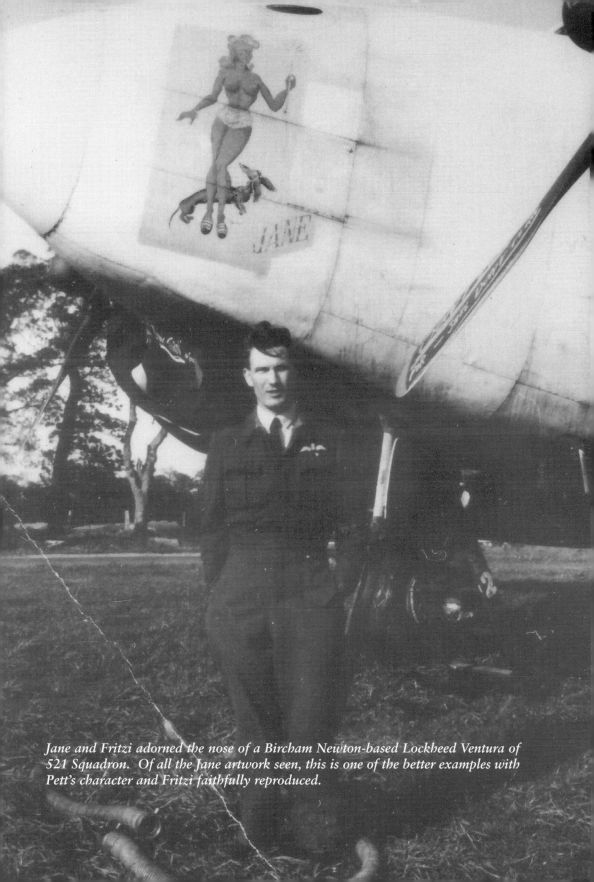

Jane and Fritzi adorned the nose of a Bircham Newton-based Lockheed Ventura of 521 Squadron. Of all the Jane artwork seen, this is one of the better examples with Pett's character and Fritzi faithfully reproduced.

"J" becoming a replacement Jane. Instead, "J" became "Johnny" carrying the figure of "Johnny Walker" after the famous Scotch Whisky label. *"After all"*, said Walter Lewis, a former 9 Squadron AC 2 Fitter, *"there was only one Jane, and although we all still loved her to bits, the aircrews – and the ground crews – were really all quite superstitious and would have been jinxed by another one on the flight line."*

Of other aeroplanes with Jane artwork there are numerous examples, including Jane and little Fritz on a Lockheed Ventura Mk V of 521 Squadron based at Bircham Newton in 1944, and a Handley Page Halifax of 462 Squadron in 1945. Post-war, and despite the initially undiminished popularity of Jane, the more relaxed attitudes of the wartime RAF had changed so that, after six years, Jane and her various comic friends were scrubbed from the fuselages of numerous surviving warplanes then still in service. Interestingly, during the 1982 Falklands conflict, a Nimrod maritime reconnaissance aircraft of 201 Squadron RAF sported a design executed by artist Neil Foggo and depicting a buxom curvy female sitting on a missile in time-honoured fashion; underneath, the inscription "Jane". It would be nice to think that this *was* Jane, our Jane, but it would probably be stretching credibility to really suggest that it was. By 1982, most memories of the *Daily Mirror*'s Jane had all but faded in the armed services of the day; but perhaps we could let ourselves believe that Foggo had been inspired by photographs of an earlier wartime Jane? Maybe. Certainly though, Nimrod XV234 seems to have been the RAF's last "Jane", although Amanda Jane appeared on Tornado ZD851 during the first Gulf War and Katrina Jane on Jaguar XZ119 in the same conflict, both featuring rather top-heavy, scantily-clad and curvy blondes. At least the tradition lived on. Well … almost!

Writing to the *Daily Mirror* from Burma, a special correspondent told of how one army unit there had a dance band: *"Its most important component was Jane – the prized double bass fiddle – so called because of her revealing curves."* Boats, tanks and planes were clearly not the only inanimate objects named after her. Another irreverent use of her name came with the clever design of a spoof unit badge for an unnamed regiment. Even the GR Royal cipher wasn't spared, JR being carefully woven into a regimental flag in the Middle East. According to legend the flag was regularly carried on parade – once during an inspection by Monty – and never discovered. It is a nice story. If true, it is probably just as well that nobody ever knew. Fun was fun after all, but Army discipline and Kings Regulations would certainly have taken a more than dim view of the disrespect to the reigning Monarch and Crown. If not The Tower then an Army "glasshouse" might certainly have loomed for the perpetrator! The originator of the crime, an unnamed Corporal, told how his defence would simply be that it was an old flag left over and simply overlooked since the time of Queen Jane who had ruled for

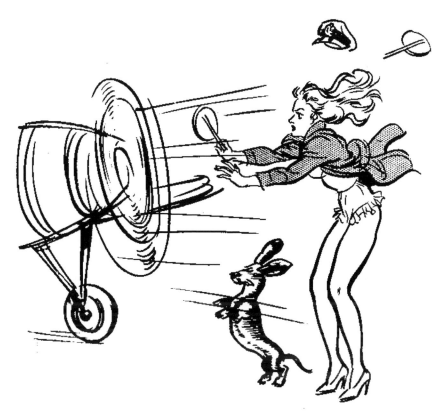

Either Norman Pett had limited technical knowledge or he was exercising artistic licence in this RAF portrayal of Jane who is suffering from the effects of a reverse-thrust propeller! This is simply one of his sketches and was not part of a cartoon strip.

fourteen days in 1554. Such was the spirit of Jane fans!

Whilst it does not need any deep analysis to reason why Jane was so popular as both pin-up and mascot, the *Picture Post* of 23 September 1944 decided to conduct what it called "An experiment in taste". The magazine described it thus:

> *"In a recent article in* Picture Post *discussing the work done by the Council for the Encouragement of Music and the Arts (CEMA) in supplying pictures to the forces, Osbert Lancaster suggested that the Council should provide pin-up girls painted by first-rate artists to compete with those culled from cinema magazines. What would be the reaction of the troops to such pictures, we asked, and in order to find the answer we commissioned Mass Observation to conduct an enquiry into the opinions of men and women at a Service Club"*

JANE IN THE N.F.S.

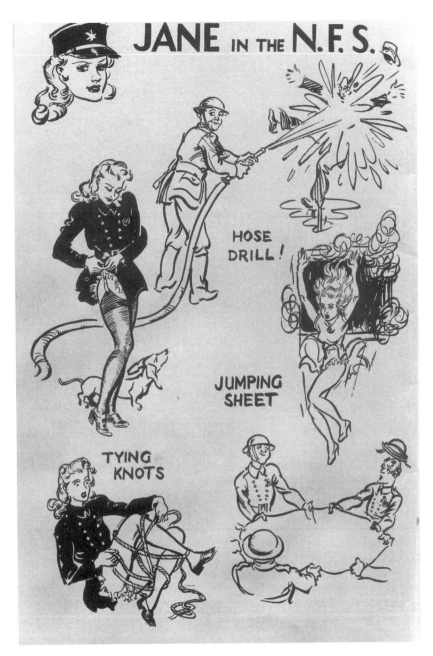

HOSE DRILL!

JUMPING SHEET

TYING KNOTS

Predominantly, Jane was very much an RAF pin-up, although she certainly appeared on tanks, trucks and ships. In much-blitzed Coventry, one NFS fire tender was named Lady Godiva and featured a scantily-clad Jane in (almost!) NFS uniform. Pett was anxious to appeal to all branches of the armed forces and civilian services. This was his NFS tribute.

90

For the purposes of this rather peculiar exercise, service personnel were asked to vote on twelve images of the female form from old masters, to cartoons and film stars – being required to mark A, B or C against the pictures of their first, second and third choice. Into this pastiche of beauties, of course, was cast our heroine Jane and it is fascinating to find that whilst a real-life image of a study of a semi-nude by photographer Roye and a portrait 'photo of Dorothy Maguire beat her into third place, she still managed to beat other images – including the one and only Betty Grable, then Hollywood's hottest pin-up! Whilst Pett was delighted with the results, they really came as no surprise, and although Betty Grable, Lana Turner and her ilk would grace many a barrack room wall, they did not translate well into the painted pin-up mascot as typified by Jane. Following on from this survey into pin-up tastes, another services quiz show asked a variety of questions about famous women. Jane, it seems, was the only female personality known to all contestants!

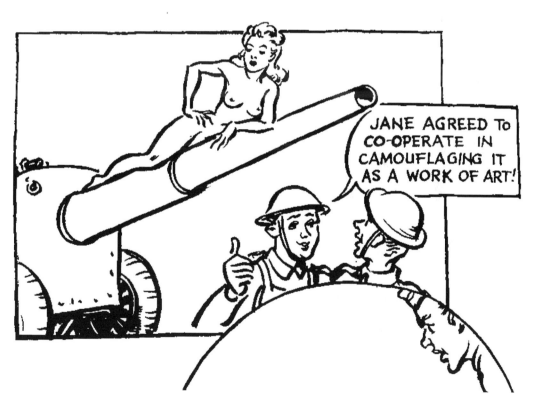

This Pett cartoon of Jane was reproduced in a wartime Army training manual. No doubt Jane helped to get the message across to an audience likely to have been less receptive to less light hearted instructional approaches!

At Wiston House in West Sussex, Canadian soldiers painted a large picture of Jane on one of the walls inside the house. Still there, Jane has been preserved although she remains hidden behind another larger framed painting. For the RAF she remained the fuselage artwork of choice, and it was a similar story with the Army. At least once, in September 1941, Jane in person (Chrystabel, that is) rode aboard a British Army Matilda tank called "Stormcock" at Bath when appearing in the Palace Theatre there. Together with Fritzi, she was photographed with admiring soldiers and civilians when she supported the Ministry of Supply's "Speed the Tanks" campaign. Judging from the reaction of the crowds there, her appearance far eclipsed its purpose. Jane was to have promoted the campaign. Instead, the tanks were just a convenient and incidental backdrop for the appearance of Britain's most glamorous

Jane and Matilda. During Bath's Speed the Tanks Week in September 1941, Chrystabel and Fritzi were photographed aboard a Matilda tank with schoolchildren and the tank crew. The children seem particularly interested in Fritzi, and the soldiers are politely appearing to be so. In reality, the troops' interest certainly lies more with Jane than with her dog!

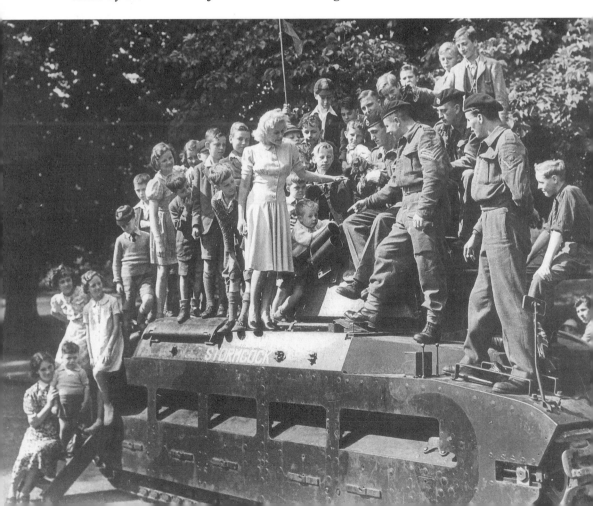

woman. Interest was focussed on her alone and, sadly, the tank campaign's purpose seemed forgotten.

When the Army could get away with it, but usually only in active combat theatres, her outline chalked on tanks and trucks was not uncommon. It is even said, although it may be an apocryphal tale, that the first British tank ashore in Normandy on D-Day was decorated with a drawing of Jane. True or not, it has passed into the folklore of World War Two and the enduring legend of Jane.

For the Navy, as we have seen, it was not exactly possible to decorate ships in such a manner – much as the matelots would have loved to do so! Mindful of the particular penchant for Jane within the Royal Navy, Norman Pett executed one particularly famous drawing showing her in a jaunty (and scanty!) sailor's outfit and with a life-jacketed Fritz. Signed 'photos, too, of Chrystabel were sent out on request to RN ships, set in a similar pose, and with an HMS Jane life belt displayed alongside for effect.

The boys of 835 Squadron, Fleet Air Arm, remained fiercely proud of Jane on the cowling of one of the squadron's Swordfish aeroplanes – that is, until the squadron flew off its carrier, HMS *Nairana*, and back to its shore base at Hatston. Here, the Commander flew into a rage when he saw Jane, the more so when her pilot explained that it was all part of ensuring that everything was *"ship-shape and Bristol fashion!"* Exploding, the said Commander retorted that he considered Jane far from ship-shaped and in the interests of decency would prefer not to comment on the Bristol part of the saying! Demonstrating at least some good humour, he finally agreed that Jane's head and shoulders could remain – everything below there must go. This was solved expeditiously by the replacement of the cowling on which Jane's lower half was painted with a spare panel. The original, meanwhile, was stowed safely and Hatston's Commander was none the wiser. Back on board the *Nairana* the panel was swiftly replaced, but frequent shore detachments back to Hatson meant, according to Fleet Air Arm Mechanic Ernie Batten, that: *"Jane's more interesting bits were on and off that aeroplane more times than she was in and out of her smalls!"*

Of all the combatants of World War Two, it was surely the submariners who had the loneliest and most dangerous of jobs – but Jane had an unusual way of easing that loneliness and detracting from the danger for these undersea sailors. Like any other mess deck, Jane could be found on any RN submarine but it was how she got there that was unique. Isolated and insulated from the outside world for weeks or months at a time, the *Daily Mirror* came up with a novel way to lift the sailors' spirits and designed and published a special newspaper called *Good Morning*. In 1945 the *Mirror* revealed how it was done:

"For 924 days – seven days a week – it has appeared, battle or calm, crisp and new at breakfast-time in every British submarine on

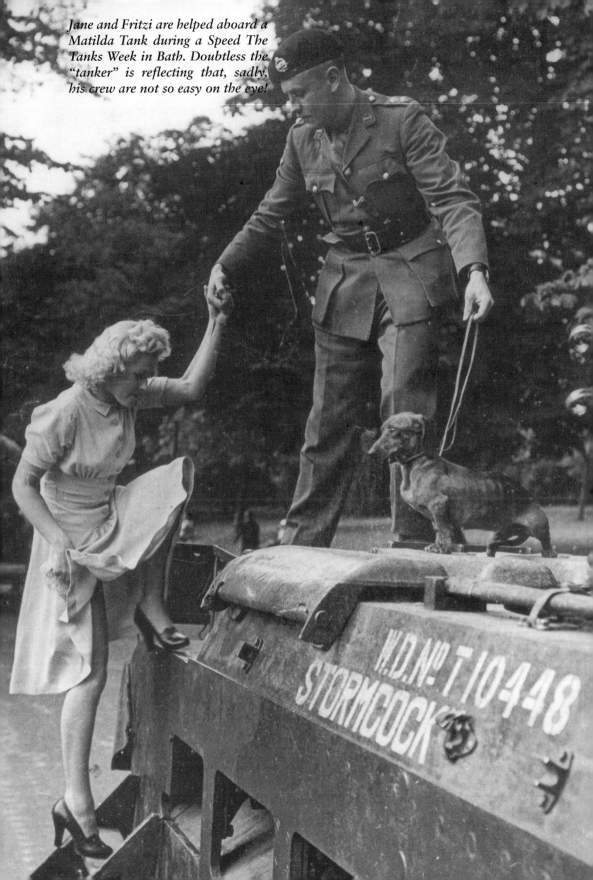

Jane and Fritzi are helped aboard a Matilda Tank during a Speed The Tanks Week in Bath. Doubtless the "tanker" is reflecting that, sadly, his crew are not so easy on the eye!

W.D. Nº T 10448

STORMCOCK

operations. Fathoms deep in mid-Atlantic ... weeks at sea in mid-Pacific ... every morning at breakfast, there it was, a Daily Mirror *tribute to the men beneath the sea. It was never seen on a news stand. How could it happen – a newspaper every morning in mid-ocean? Like this. It was obviously impossible to send it out daily. So it was dispatched from the printers in batches of twenty-eight days' issues at a time.*

A whole month's newspapers, with six copies of every day's newspaper for every British submarine – parcelled up and sent to the Admiralty – then quickly labelled for individual boats and rushed away to the GPO.

Whisked off by air all over the world to the bases for which the ships beneath the sea were making – Gibraltar, Malta, Colombo, Fremantle ...

As the submarines glided in, the parcels were rushed from the 'plane – eagerly loaded, safely stowed.

Then, daily at sea as the dawn watch ended, the coxswain took six copies of the day's paper and distributed them around the messes. No issue was dated. Every one was numbered.

It was not red hot news, but it was what the submariners wanted – news from their own homes – intimately, exclusively for them. A picture of Bill's new baby that he'd never seen; a word about how old Charlie's tomatoes were doing; or a photo of Edna's wedding.

Full page pin-ups followed, and the old familiar strip cartoons – the adventures of Jane were frequently seen under the sea well in advance of their appearance in this country."

And so it was that a special relationship, a unique bond, was developed between the submarine crews and Jane. So much so that when one of HM submarines became stranded on the sea bed after being depth-charged, special measures were taken by the Captain to raise morale ... break open the newspapers to find out what Jane was up to. The *Daily Mirror* later took up the story:

"The engines were dead. There was only quiet, and that high-pitched singing in the ears that rose as the boat slowly went down.

Inside the submarine, there was the strange, tense atmosphere of men perhaps about to die, slowly, quietly and alone.

Then the coxswain came round. With him he had a large parcel. One by one he peeled them off – tomorrow ... and tomorrow ... and tomorrow. The tomorrows they did not expect to see.

Three weeks of papers all at once. There was no point in wasting them.

Eagerly they raced through Jane – three weeks ahead of London.

Then suddenly, the sound of an engine throbbing. The engineers had won. A cheer went up.

Jane had got them through, they were convinced of it."

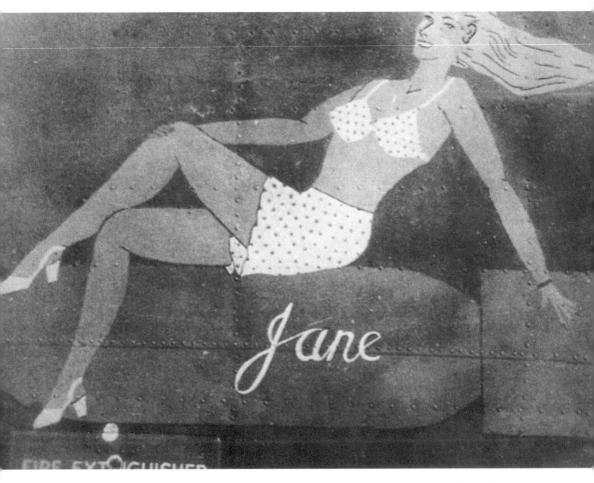

American examples of Jane being carried on USAAF or USN aircraft are known to have existed, but were rare. This was a rendition applied to a B-24 Liberator of the 446th Bomb Group. Typically, a scantily-clad Jane rides a bomb.

The closeness of the submarine community was unique to the armed services, and the closeness of the submariners to Jane was unequalled as this story reveals. As for the crew of HM Submarine *Tally-Ho!*, captained by Commander Bennington DSO DSC, they traditionally chalked and painted a small Jane onto the conning tower side each time prior to the first dive after leaving port, perhaps the only Royal Navy boat so decorated. Superstition had it that if Jane's underwear hadn't washed off by the time they next surfaced then they were in for a bad run of luck. Leading Stoker Jim Phillpot was usually the artist, and mindful of the bad luck implications for the ship he later confided that he always made sure that Jane herself was in relatively fast paints and the underwear in very soluble chalks! As if to underscore the special relationship between the submariners and Jane, one submarine officer produced an oil portrait of Jane and Fritzi during a long stint at sea and later presented it to Chrystabel. It became one of her most treasured possessions.

Army, Navy and Air Force, and each branch of each of those services, all took Jane to heart in their own way. Echoing Jane's multifarious military allegiances, Norman Pett ensured that he drew her wearing (or not wearing!) the uniforms of each of His Majesty's Services – not to mention organisations like the Womens' Land Army, Civil Defence or Ambulance Service. Indeed, it would not be surprising to discover that some tractor, rescue tender or ambulance in wartime Britain had also been named after Jane. In fact, it would be more surprising if one of them hadn't!

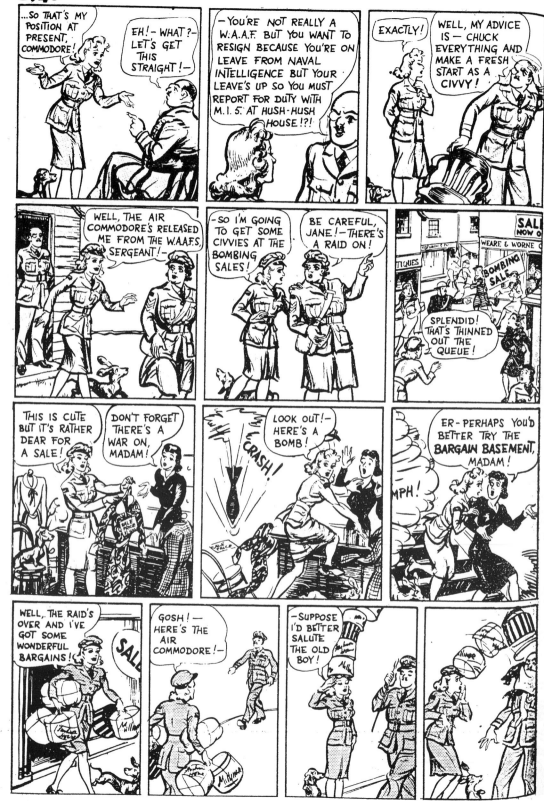

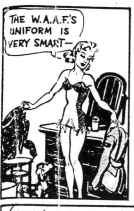

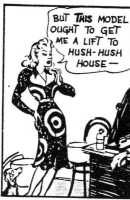

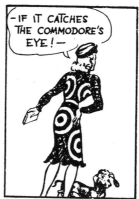

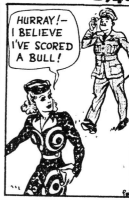

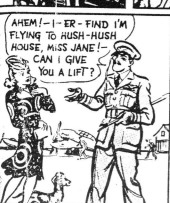

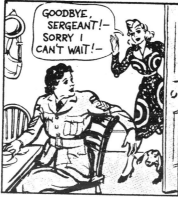

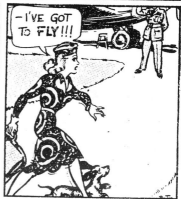

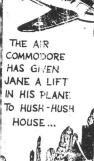

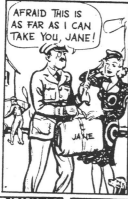

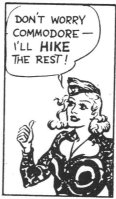

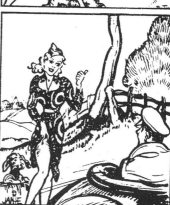

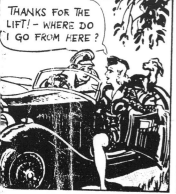

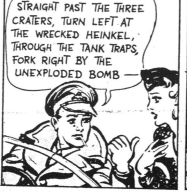

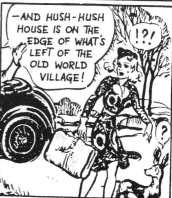

Chapter Seven

I Remember Jane!

There could not have been many British servicemen who did not remember Jane. Perhaps to each she meant something different, but of all the other servicemen worldwide who had cause to fondly remember her, perhaps the most unusual was the German war correspondent and photographer Walter Doelfs who had been attached to the Luftwaffe and based in Holland. In 1949, he tracked down Norman Pett and wrote to him about his own particular memory:

> "Today, exactly seven years ago, it happened that I made acquaintance with your Jane. I was near Leeuwarden in Holland. The matter of this acquaintance was a sad one though, because it cost the lives of some of your young men who were the most ardent admirers of Jane.
>
> "On the night of 21 June 1942, an RAF Wellington was shot down by the Luftwaffe nightfighter ace Oberleutnant Prinz zur Lippe-Weissenfeld, holder of the Knights Cross, and who was later shot down himself. After we had buried the RAF men with full military honours we interested ourselves in the wreck of the Wellington. There, standing proudly on the nose of the bomber, was your really pretty Jane who through some miracle had survived the crash. Unhurt, she stood before us – scantily clad and beautiful. As we approached she seemed to smile at us. We couldn't believe our eyes. Bouncing around her was her little dog who was also unhurt and I wonder if you can imagine our joy at this charming meeting? In the midst of all the bloody happenings of war and a murderous air battle, here was Jane.
>
> "When Prinz zur Lippe-Weissenfeld saw this strange victim of his 27th night victory, his eyes lit up. It was the first time we had been able to persuade him to look at one of the aeroplanes he had shot down, because he didn't like to be reminded of the men he had had to kill. But when this 23-year-old flyer from Salzburg saw Jane he was smitten. "If she were real I'd marry her straight away!" he told us. But she was only out of a paint tin, although he was not prepared to forsake her. Instead, he had her cut out of the fuselage along with her name, her dog and the fifteen bombs which showed how many times she had been to Germany. He then ordered a frame and had her hung on the Officers' Mess wall where she was proudly shown to all

visitors. Even the most important visitors saw her and once she actually met Herman Goering! One day, Prinz zur Lippe-Weissenfeld asked me to take a photograph of him posing with his Jane. Everyone who saw this photo wanted one and I had to make hundreds of them – but who this Jane was, nobody had the slightest idea and we hadn't heard of the Daily Mirror. And until yesterday I myself had not the slightest idea who Jane was either.

"Imagine this coincidence. Today, on 21 June 1949, exactly seven years after I first met Jane, I found an edition of the German

The reverse of the same photograph with its caption. Translated, it reads:
"Jane, the scantily-dressed British fliers' sweetheart, has discovered a better role than that of decorating the fuselage of a British nightbomber.
"Oberleutnant zur Lippe shows her off to his visitors, as a trophy from his twenty-seventh nightfighter victory".

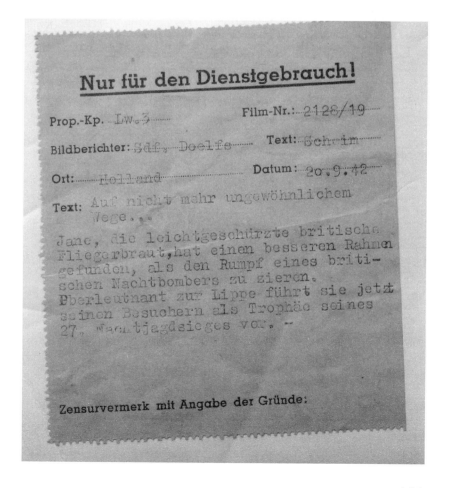

magazine Revue. *There, on page eleven, I found the story of Jane's creation by you and a picture of her wearing that same pretty costume just like on our Wellington bomber and with the same little dog that had accompanied her on her nightly trips to Germany. When I saw this Jane I quickly fetched my suitcase of pictures from the loft and found the photograph. Today I am sending it to you in remembrance of those young men who died in Jane's Wellington."*

Of all those with reasons to remember Jane, Walter Doelfs' memory must have been the most poignant. But that is not to say that other memories were any the less significant to those holding them. Whether they be memories of the cartoon strip itself or of stage shows, personal

One of the more unusual reminiscences about Jane came from Luftwaffe war photographer Walter Doelfs. On 21 June 1942, an RAF 9 Squadron Wellington was shot down over Holland with the loss of its entire crew, including the Squadron Commander, Squadron Leader James. Doelfs photographed the victor, Oblt. Prinz zur Lippe–Weissenfeld, posing with the Jane artwork panel from the Wellington. Several years after the War, Doelfs discovered who Jane and her little dog actually were. Tracking down Norman Pett, he sent him a touching letter and this original photograph.

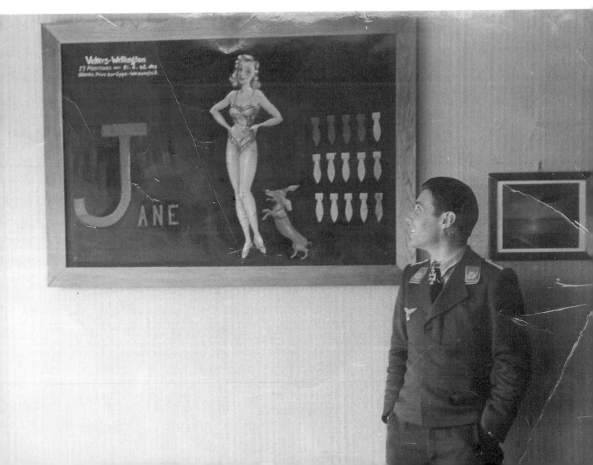

appearances or through some other connection to Jane, there must have been as many memories as there were serving personnel in the British forces during World War Two. Whatever, the impact of those memories has endured. Incredibly, after more than fifty years many seemed to remember, unprompted, some of the storylines of the cartoon strip and many of the drawings themselves. What other cartoon, one wonders, can have ever had such an impression? An imponderable question, too, is whatever *was* the magic of Jane that created such a sensation? Perhaps we shall never know, and perhaps it is futile to attempt to find answers to these questions. Instead, let us enjoy a few of those fondly-held memories recorded for posterity by some of her many fans.

For some, Jane became a means of communication between loved ones – either just for fun or, as in the case of Trooper Frank Ottley, with a rather more purposeful intent:

> *"When I went abroad in 1942, I was anxious to continue my practice of writing to my wife every day but this became impossible during periods when we were in action. So, I decided to take advantage of the single sheet letter we could write which were then photographed and airmailed. Aerographs, I think they were called. Because I wouldn't have the time to write a letter when we were up at the front I instead spent all my spare time doing drawings of Jane in pencil on to the airmail sheet. At times I would have thirty or more drawings in stock. Then, if I didn't have the chance to write, I'd just send one of my girls and my wife would know that I was safe and well at that date at least. I was always surprised that the Army Postal Service accepted them on the grounds that it might be used as a method of passing secret information but I sent two or three hundred and I think nearly all arrived safely. For me, Jane became an important means of communication."*

For others, the connection with home was just as important – but for very different reasons. At the *Stalag Luft* III Prisoner of War Camp in Sagan, air gunner Richard Dewhurst remembered how one prisoner's wife or girlfriend copied out, in miniature, the Jane strip cartoons. Much missed by the POWs, these little bits of home were eagerly awaited and did the rounds of just about every prisoner in the camp. Copied and re-copied, there were not many bunk spaces that did not display Jane in all her glory. Unimpressed, the Camp Commandant ordered that any naked Janes should be clothed immediately or removed as they offended the guards! "Like hell they did!", said Dewhurst. "Every day the Goons trooped through our huts and were probably more interested in our art gallery than how many prisoners were there." The day of the cover-up order and hundreds of dresses and uniforms were cut out of paper, suitably coloured and simply pinned or hooked in place over Jane,

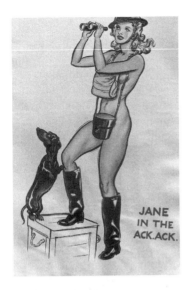

JANE
IN THE
ACK.ACK.

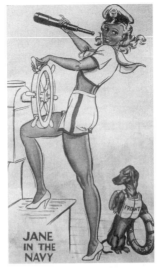

JANE
IN THE
NAVY

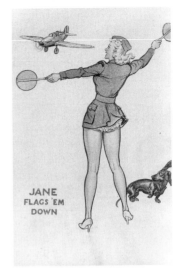

JANE
FLAGS 'EM
DOWN

Thursday, July 27, 1939

Jane . . .

All characters in this strip are fictitious and
are not intended to represent any person living
or dead. (Copyright in all countries.)

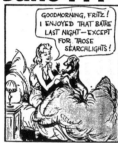

GOODMORNING, FRITZ!
I ENJOYED THAT BATHE
LAST NIGHT—EXCEPT
FOR THOSE
SEARCHLIGHTS!

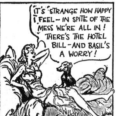

IT'S STRANGE HOW HAPPY
I FEEL—IN SPITE OF THE
MESS WE'RE ALL IN!
THERE'S THE HOTEL
BILL—AND BASIL'S
A WORRY!

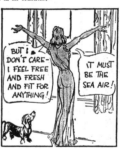

BUT I
DON'T CARE—
I FEEL FREE
AND FRESH
AND FIT FOR
ANYTHING!

IT MUST
BE THE
SEA AIR!

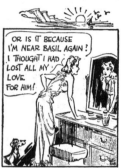

OR IS IT BECAUSE
I'M NEAR BASIL AGAIN?
I THOUGHT I HAD
LOST ALL MY
LOVE
FOR HIM!

*To appeal to all the services, Pett often did drawings upon request that he dedicated
to specific units, ships or regiments. These three were for the Army, Navy and Air
Force with another being of a topical home-front subject. Pett often used and re-used
particular poses. Compare the "blackout Jane" in her diaphanous nightie on the
next page to this particular strip cartoon frame.*

leaving the possibility of undressing her out of the Goons' prying eyes.
Knowing that the Goons would look, Dewhust drew in a bikini with
swastikas over each nipple and a caricature of Hitler's face on her bikini
bottom. It worked. Purple with rage, *Gefreiter* Schiller confiscated the
offending Jane – only for another friendly guard to confide to Dewhurst
that Jane now had new quarters in the German barracks where her Nazi
underwear apparently continued to cause great hilarity. The Führer,
most probably, would have been less amused! For Dewhurst and his
pals, Jane was considered a life saver during some pretty bleak times.

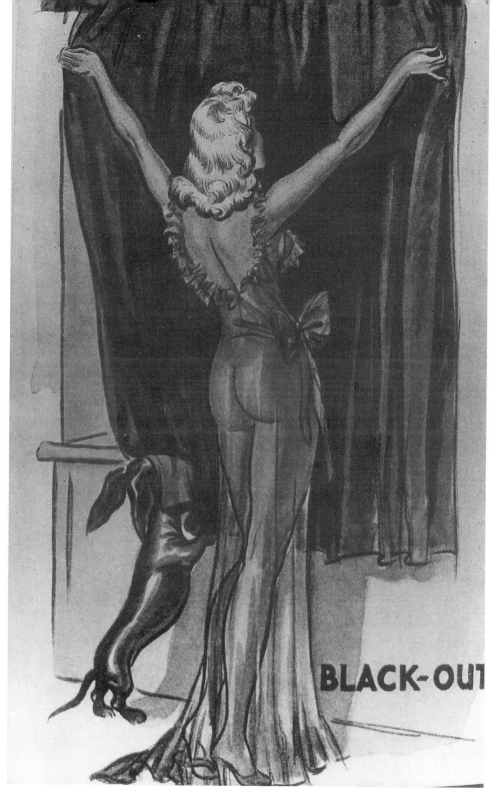

The "blackout Jane" in question.

Warrant Officer "Tommy" Thompson though, ashore on D-Day with the Royal Engineers, quite literally had his life saved by Jane. Under fierce German machine-gun fire, he was pinned down with his troop on the beachhead. Thompson took up the story for himself:

"All hell had broken loose and I was laying face down in the sand and water. Bullets were kicking up the muck all around me and whanging off metal obstacles and vehicles. Above the noise of explosions there was a lot of yelling and shouting from boys who had been hit. I eventually tried to get up to move to cover, but was knocked to the ground straight away and winded. I looked down and saw a big hole in the left breast of my battledress tunic. My chest was sore and red, but there was no blood. I crawled behind a knocked out tank and took stock. I had been hit right over the heart, but the bullet had been stopped by my hand-made cigarette case and Ronson lighter that were both just about wrapped into a ball with a bent bullet inside the case. The cigarette case was only aluminium and had been made by Italian PoWs. What was special about it was that it had an engraving of Jane and Fritzi on it and was a gift from my girlfriend – also a Jane! Although only quite flimsy it had absorbed the impact. Being right-handed it is just natural to put things in your left top pocket so that, and Jane, had saved my life. I regret to say that I ended up leaving it on the beach because, as I lay there winded and shocked, it and everything else fell out of my shredded tunic. Then we moved out in a hurry, and Jane my saviour stayed on the Normandy beach somewhere near Ouistreham. Jane truly saved my life that day."

Later, and certainly by August 1944, Thompson recalled a Rest & Recuperation centre in France for British troops. There, inside a large marquee, was situated "Jane's Café", the walls festooned with original Pett artwork of Jane that had been specially commissioned and sent out to France. Many of them had been dedicated by Pett to certain units or regiments, and all of them signed by Jane. Needless to say, it wasn't long before quite a few started to vanish and eventually the Military Police started a search of kit bags and trucks where most of the liberated drawings were located. (One of these, at least, escaped the trawl and turned up in a London auction house during the late nineteen eighties where it raised a fairly considerable sum.)

Not so fortunate as "Tommy" Thompson was twenty-one year old Spitfire pilot, Sgt Frederick Nelson. Serving with 616 Squadron and operating out of RAF Tangmere, he was killed when his Spitfire spun into the ground after returning from an operational flight on 21 July 1941. When his body was extricated from the wreckage near Bognor Regis, a poignant discovery was made in his uniform tunic pocket. The find was detailed in a list of personal effects that were to be sent home and that had been drawn up by the squadron adjutant:

> *"One portrait photograph, sepia, of young lady in bathing costume. Badly torn and damaged. Signed to Frederick with love from Jane of the* Daily Mirror.*"*

Quite likely, Jane's photograph was with hundreds – if not thousands – of British servicemen when they made that ultimate sacrifice. As Chrystabel later said, she was, after all, "... everyone's girlfriend."

For Ron Parker, there is a rather more permanent reminder and memory of Jane than was the case with many servicemen. Too young to serve in the war, he nevertheless followed Jane's exploits in the *Daily Mirror*, and when his time for National Service arrived in 1949 it was also time, as with many other lads of the same age, to get a tattoo. Stationed in Aldershot, it was a case of off to Jess's Tattoo Parlour, where a splendid figure of Jane was emblazoned on his upper arm in red and blue. Scantily clad (of course!) the tattoo caused as much outrage for Parker's mother as it had some years earlier to the *Stalag Luft* III Commandant and she promptly pronounced it "Disgusting!" and ordered Ron "Go and cover her up at once!" He didn't, and over fifty years later Jane the tattoo lived on.

For Ron Whitelaw, service in the RAF also saw him gain a lasting and tangible reminder of Jane dating from his posting to the Orkneys. On Christmas Day 1940, a Junkers 88 was shot down by the Fleet Air Arm and made a crash landing at Sandwick on Loch Skaie. The crew were all captured and the 'plane souvenired by locals and the troops. Later, Whitelaw secured a large lump of clear perspex from the bomber's cockpit canopy and fashioned his trophy into the figure of Jane with her little Fritz. The end result was a lovely piece of period ornamentation – or what has loosely been termed "Trench Art" in more recent years. The perspex Jane has endured the years well. More than sixty years later she still adorned Ron's window sill where she continued to draw many admiring glances.

The Navy, too, had its memories and Charlie Lancaster's recollection is almost redolent of the later "Navy Lark" comedy broadcasts on the BBC Light Programme. It also involved yet another cover-up order!

> *"I was serving as signaller on a Tank Landing Ship (LST) and being rather artistic my skipper gave me a free hand to brighten the ship. I soon got cracking and painted everything in sight. This, however, did not please the Flotilla Commander who, after a ship inspection, told us our LST looked like "...a bloody Italian Ice Cream cart". Not to be dismayed, I set forth in the wheelhouse and on all four walls painted cartoon characters – Popeye, Belinda, Donald Duck and Jane in pride of place in front of the wheel and right across the bulkhead.*

How this pleased our coxswain! He could admire Jane's nude figure while steering the ship, but this coincided with a series of mishaps.

" "Out fenders!" would be the panicky cry from the bridge as we came crashing alongside our berth. Was the ship actually going to port when the skipper rang down "Starboard"?

"Came the day of reckoning. The skipper entered the wheelhouse, looked around, and his gaze settled on the nude Jane. Then came the command we dreaded. Jane must go. She was distracting the Cox from his duties, but in the end our skipper was human after all and allowed me to suitably attire her in (almost) respectable underwear."

Another naval reflection came from Fleet Air Arm Mechanic Bert Dyer:

"In 1944 or '45 I was just nineteen years old and on leave in my home town of Bristol. One Friday night, my cousin and I attended a variety show at the Empire Theatre in Old Market Street. Jane was top of the bill and I can't remember any of the other acts. We were sat about three rows back in the front stalls. Jane's act, which she must have perfected by doing it so many times, started with just her outlined by a spotlight on a white screen, getting dressed and then appearing in scanty but tasteful clothes as she came down into the audience. She came straight to our row of seats, picked me out and took me by the hand and politely asked me to come up onto the stage with her. Jane put her arms around me, and my arms about her, so that we were close together and face to face whilst she sang me a little song – although I cannot remember what it was. I was so very, very nervous, but Jane was a real lady.

"After the show, cousin Bob and I were walking home in the black-out when he asked what it was like being up on stage with Jane. I said that all I could remember were my hot hands on her bare back. At that moment, a Policeman stepped out of the gloom. All he could have heard was my reply to Bob, and I could see his big grin: "'Cor, luvverly!" he exclaimed.

"I suppose my stage story must have been repeated by hundreds of servicemen, but the next morning I was out in town with my father, when who should we see but Jane walking towards us with her Fritzi. "Good morning!" she said cheerily. She had remembered me! My Dad just stood there, rooted to the spot!"

Immediately after VJ Day, the Royal Navy began a campaign of "showing the flag" around Britain's coast, visiting various ports and seaside towns. On board HMS *Zephyr* was Leading Seaman Jim Crutchlow:

"One week we visited Grimsby, and while we were there word was put out that we would be getting a VIP visitor. Just before midday, we

seamen were all at Quarters Clean Guns with me in charge of the Bridge party. Suddenly, a car drew up alongside on the quay, the door opened and out poked Jane's great legs. She climbed the brow, stood at its head and waved and smiled to the ship's entire company, now wolf-whistling like mad. She called out "Hello boys!" and a great cry went up: "JANE!" Then, she slowly went up to the wardroom for drinks, bless her. It must have been the one and only time that a woman improperly dressed in a bathing costume was invited to the wardroom – but the Captain didn't seem to mind that much! Later, before she left the ship, she toured around having photos taken with various crew members".

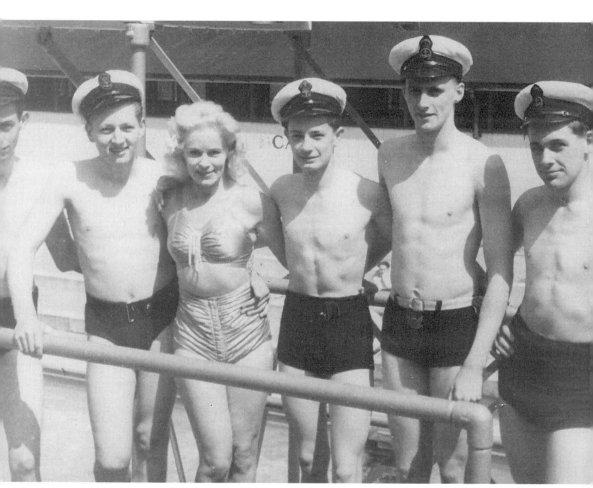

Jane cheers the Navy. This picture was taken aboard HMS Zephyr when Chrystabel visited the ship shortly after VJ Day at Grimsby and posed with this group of Petty Officers.

Memories of Jane, however, were not solely the province of servicemen. Schoolboy Leon Bloom was eleven years old and a pupil at a school in Hove, East Sussex, during the last two years of the war. He takes up the story:

"I hated maths and algebra with a passion. Art was really my forté, and it got me into a lot of trouble. Bored, I drew a little figure of Jane inside the cover of my exercise book. Although I say so myself, it was rather good. I thought it was pretty well hidden, but I didn't reckon on the eagle eye of our master, Mr Turkington – Turkey to us boys of course. Turkey took me to one side and gave me an embarrassing lecture on female immodesty and lust. Both deadly sins, he told me. As a punishment, I had to write out the ten commandments twenty times, I think. Well, at that time we were in the middle of Flying Bomb attacks. As soon as one was seen or heard approaching it was a mad dash into the shelter. One day we were herded by Turkey into our concrete tunnel. As we got used to the light, there on the wall was a full-size rendering of Jane in charcoal and absolutely starkers. As the doodlebug droned its lethal way overhead I shall never forget the sight of Turkey standing up and holding his gown, Batman fashion, to shield Jane from our eager young eyes. On the way out of the shelter he boomed "Bloom, my study. NOW!" I protested my innocence, but to no avail. I was a good artist and had already been caught drawing Jane. Although I had never seen our charcoal Jane before that day, I was guilty as charged and caned severely. The worst part was that I then got beaten by my father when he discovered my alleged misdemeanour! Oddly, nobody scrubbed out the charcoal Jane and so I crept back to have an admiring lascivious peek whenever I could. Having been punished for her I sure as hell was going to make it as worthwhile as possible! I never did find out who really drew her, but let my friends believe it was me. You have no idea how much kudos – street cred in today's terminology – that this gave me. I never knew for sure, but suspected the groundsman was the real artist!"

Corporal Frank McKechnie of 1st Battalion The Rifle Brigade recalls four half-track vehicles in his platoon. *"One of the chaps could draw, so on the back of each truck he painted different scenes – Jane getting ready for a bath, standing by the bath in bra and panties, undressing and then in the bath. We had a lot of fun watching peoples' faces as they saw us go past, waiting for the next picture to come along! We had them through D-Day and after, but then we had to paint them out before we were inspected by Monty. A sad day, that!"*

Sometimes, Jane herself became a casualty of the war and former Able Seaman Knowling had to leave her to go on her way to the bottom of the

Barents Sea when his ship, HMS *Cassandra*, was torpedoed off the North Cape. Sixty-five of his shipmates went down with the *Cassandra*, and Knowling was lucky to escape with his life. Surviving with just the clothes he was stood up in, Knowling was filled with an almost unbearable sadness at the loss of his friends. As for his kit, that could be replaced – but on his locker had been a signed photo of Jane and of all of his lost possessions, this was the loss – aside from his mates – that he admitted he felt most keenly. It was as if Jane herself had gone to the bottom, and the affect on his morale, he recalled, was out of all proportion to reality. It demonstrated, though, the importance to many of Jane the mascot or good luck talisman. Without Jane, Knowling feared he would not survive the war. Luckily he did survive, but he still remembered more than fifty years later the total fear of going to sea again without his Jane. Even an eventual replacement was no substitute for Knowling.

The aftermath of D-Day in the Normandy countryside as Royal Marines dig in alongside crumpled Airspeed Horsa troop-carrying gliders. At Pegasus Bridge, Major Howard recalled the commotion caused when bundles of the Daily Mirror *were dropped on 7 June and the scramble amongst the troops to see what Jane had been up to.*

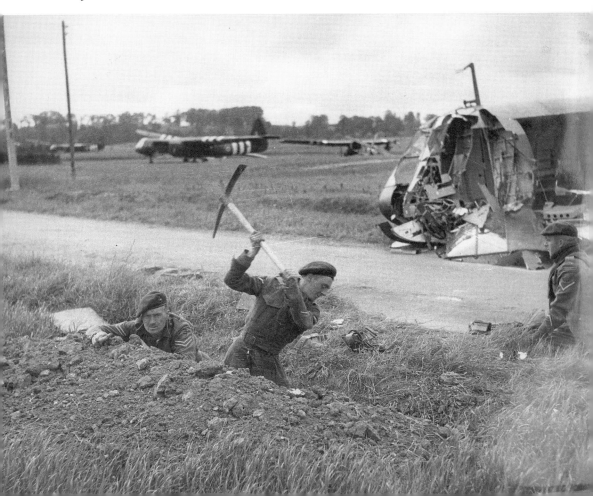

A similar memory to McKechnie's comes from Derek Holmes, formerly of the Royal Engineers (Heavy Section) who took Jane to Normandy on D-Day, 6 June 1944. The truck he drove had a life-size sunbathing Jane, nude, chalked across the top front of the cab. Neither the salt spray of the Channel, nor the rain and mud of Normandy, could do anything to wash Jane out of the picture. Derek later recalled that she drew many an impressed wolf-whistle across France for several months after the landings.

For the 8th Leicestershire Regiment, as with many service units, Jane became their official mascot, finding time, through the good offices of Chrystabel, to write and send photographs out to the men. One of the signed 'photos travelled with the 8th Leicesters' John Emson through the battles of North Africa and Italy before being "borrowed" from him by a GI from the US Fifth Army. Peeved at its loss, John was still able to

GREAT ARMADA STRETCHED OVER HORIZON

JOHN HOGAN, *your own correspondent with the Merchant Navy, yesterday cabled this picture of the immense convoy fleet on the eve of the historic D-Day.*

THE guns have been finally checked, and the ship's locks on board synchronised. Everything is now ready for the signal to hoist anchor and sail with our cargo of men, ammunition, petrol and mines.

Months of preparations have ended. This is invasion eve.

Imagine the biggest lake you now plastered with bobbing autumn leaves and you have a picture of what I can see from

the salt-sprayed bridge of our ship.

Everywhere on the sea are steel ships. You can't get anywhere without seeing long lines of troopships, supply vessels, assault craft and warships — stretching away to faint blobs on the horizon.

Within sight of green fields and houses that draw their black-outs at dusk, one of the great Allied invasion fleets is assembled — just one of several along Britain's coast.

Swarming over every ship are khaki-men and dungareed seamen. At the docksides are thousands more troops, loaded with their kits and in rare good humour.

Dozens of soldiers swarm over the decks of this coaster. They live in a huge canvas tent on the deck.

Brown tents are to be seen everywhere. Sleek warships are alongside us, and minesweepers stretch out on the port side.

How have the soldiers and seamen spent their last leisure hours without newspapers, or the privilege of writing to the women and children from whom they have disappeared?

They have turned the ship into a fun fair.

John Fuller, of Anlaby-road, Hull, a big husky seaman of 20, has skippered a comic football team on the battered forward hold.

I asked Fuller, the Tommy Trinder of the crew, how he felt about setting sail in a couple of hours.

"Me? bloody champion I feel. I can't get there soon enough."

For Jack Upperton, of South View-road, Southwick,

Essex, the invasion will satisfy a curiosity born off the beaches of Dunkirk, when he brought back 1,560 men, and was machine-gunned by German E-boats.

Nearly all the soldiers have shaved.

"Damn it, we must make ourselves presentable when we call on Jerry," explained one.

Midships I found a corporal painting a girl's name on the back of the leather jerkin of Private Kenneth Linley. It was the name of Linley's wife. They were married five weeks ago

The soldiers are singing. . . .

"O God, our help in ages past." Quietly at first, then louder.

That was invasion eve on board one of the 4,000 ships which yesterday ferried a great army to strike at Hitler in France. The soldiers who played comic football on her decks are now in the greatest game of all.

JANE . . .

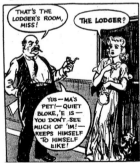
THAT'S THE LODGER'S ROOM, MISS!
THE LODGER?
YUS — MA'S PET! — QUIET BLOKE, 'E IS — YOU DON'T SEE MUCH OF 'IM! — KEEPS HIMSELF TO HIMSELF LIKE!

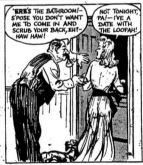
'ERE'S THE BATHROOM! — S'POSE YOU DON'T WANT ME TO COME IN AND SCRUB YOUR BACK, EH! — HAW HAW!
NOT TONIGHT, PA! — I'VE A DATE WITH THE LOOFAH!

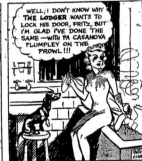
WELL, I DON'T KNOW WHY THE LODGER WANTS TO LOCK HIS DOOR, FRITZ, BUT I'M GLAD I'VE DONE THE SAME — WITH PA CASANOVA PLUMPLEY ON THE PROWL!!!

And this is what they saw. For the first time, Jane appeared in the nude – a momentous event in newspaper publishing history and in the development of Jane the strip cartoon. The strip that teased had become the cartoon that stripped!

look back fondly to her show, Hi-Diddle-Diddle at the Aldershot Hippodrome in 1941, and continued to treasure the programme for the performance of 13 October. *"The main thing"*, recalled Emson, *"was that Jane got me through some pretty hairy North African and Italian battles, bless her. I just told myself that she'd gone on a well-deserved leave when I didn't get her back from that Yank. Perhaps, like so many other English girls, he took her back home to his ranch!"*

Like Emson, Walter Hacksey was with the Army in Tunisia during 1943, when he managed to liberate Jane from the enemy at Medjes-el-Bab. Advancing into a badly knocked about village, Hacksey's platoon took some dugouts where, pinned to a wall, was a cut out cartoon strip of Jane. The ground had changed hands a few times already, so Jane had evidently amused the British and Germans alike before her final liberation. The Italians, too, met Jane in a village called Minturno as the Allied advance was held up below Monte Cassino. Here, by courtesy of the artistic George Blain serving with the Royal Corps of Signals, the whitewashed walls of his troops' basement billet were decorated with a variety of chalked murals depicting Jane, her smile easing the tension caused by incoming German artillery shells. Each bed space had a different Jane, and when time came for the troop to move off, George heard that the local Italians had fought over the occupancy of that particular room. As we have seen, replication of Pett's famous Jane artwork was widespread amongst all the armed forces but it was probably Jane in the flesh, so to speak, that for very good reason evoked the most vivid of memories.

Chrystabel Leighton-Porter's stage appearances as Jane (see Chapter 4: Jane on Stage) left many lasting impressions. Notable amongst them were the recollections of Frank Taylor who had been serving on Coastal Defence with the Army at Boscombe during the latter part of the war. Jane was appearing live on stage in Bournemouth, but Frank had been confined to barracks due to some minor misdemeanour that had infringed Kings Regulations. Desperate to get to the show, he sneaked out of camp, headed for the theatre and managed to settle himself in the dark somewhere near the front row. Towards the finale of the show, Jane came down into the auditorium and sat on one or two laps and gave out a few treasured kisses. Inevitably, Jane picked Frank to sing to and all the spotlights in the house were trained on him as he stood gazing at his heroine. Then, panic and shock set in. His eyes, accustomed now to the bright lights, settled on a whole row of familiar faces – all the Officers and NCOs of his unit! He just wanted the floor to swallow him up. *"I got another 28 days for that"*, he recalled. *"But it was worth it"*.

For his hard-earned pocket money, fifteen-year-old Colin Butchers also thought Jane was worth it. Skulking off from the Youth Club in the very early post-war years, Colin and a young pal crept into Brighton's

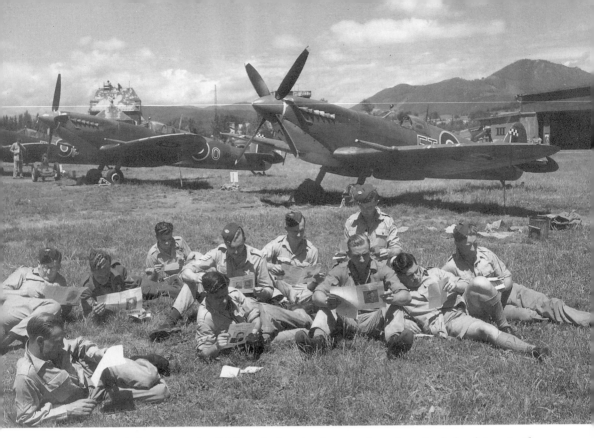

It was said that not only did Jane help win the war, but that she helped to win the 1945 General Election as well. With the majority of servicemen keen followers of Jane, they were clearly susceptible to the message of the Labour Party promoted by the Daily Mirror. *In a sense it is certainly true that Jane was a contributory factor in Churchill losing that election. Here, RAF airmen study voting papers from home at Klagenfurt, Austria, in 1945. These same servicemen had most probably followed Jane in the* Daily Mirror *and may well have been influenced in how they voted from what they had read. For the first time in history, a cartoon had had a major impact on the election of a government!*

Grand Theatre where Jane topped the bill. Both lads sat impatiently through her song and dance routine and couldn't wait for what they had come to see – the removal of her clothing! Colin recalled:

> *"In the last few seconds of her act, she removed the last wisp of clothing and stood absolutely still in the spotlight before every light in the house was extinguished. Blink at the wrong time and 3/6d would have been wasted!"*

On the way home the two boys excitedly discussed the show.

> *"Much as we were grateful to Jane for having shared her glorious femininity with us, we both concluded that she was far too old for us. She must have been 28 or 30 at the time. Oh, we had so much to learn!"*

It was the servicemen, though, for whom Jane's stage appearances held such hot appeal and, of course, enduring memory. For twenty-year-old Able Seaman Walter Cox the visit of his ship HMS *Brixham* to West Hartlepool held nostalgic memories:

> "The Empire Theatre in the town reserved the first two rows of seats for all the Naval personnel of the six minesweepers in our flotilla. As part of her show, Jane invited one of us to go up on stage with her. Sitting in the front row I was pushed off my seat and with a cheer from the two rows of sailors I was pulled up onto the stage by Jane. With my arms around her she sang to me as Fritz her dog barked his disapproval but with her tight fitting dress, and my arms around her, it made my day."

The barking dog became very much a part of Chrystabel's routine. Fritz, the tiny Dachshund, had an inbuilt dislike of men, and, at the point in the show when a male member of the audience was invited onto the stage, the dog's handler would release Fritz from the wings just as Jane embraced and kissed the chosen lucky stooge. Fritz would race onto the stage barking and snarling angrily at the serviceman, to the delight of the audience. It had all started by accident but was, of course, kept in all of the subsequent shows as part of the act. Sadly, that particular Fritz (there were several) was eventually run over by a car and none of his successors would oblige with the same performance.

For civilians, even post-war, there were those with cause to remember. Coalman Roy Voice's memory was perhaps more than a little unusual. He delivered coal to the Leighton-Porters' Sussex home and looked forward to those deliveries. The coal shed was just past the bedroom window, where Roy could always espy the famous Jane frillies neatly laid out on the bed. On a good day, Jane would be sunbathing in the garden. *"On those occasions"*, said Roy, *"you'd be quite surprised how long it took to deliver a ton of coal!"*

Soldier, sailor, airman or civilian – all had their own and widely differing memories and particular reasons to remember her. For all of them it is true to say that Jane helped make the war that much more bearable. As one old soldier put it, as he spoke fondly of Jane: *"It wasn't all bloodshed, boredom and booze ... there were distractions."*

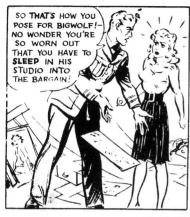

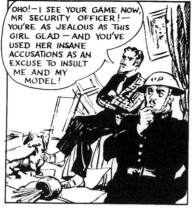

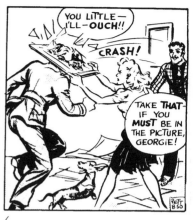

MONDAY MARCH 1

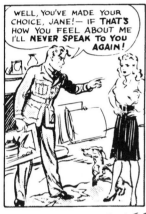

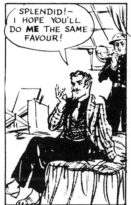

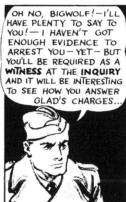

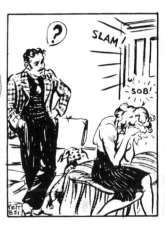

TUESDAY MARCH 2

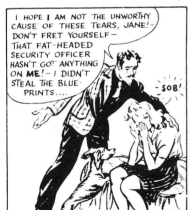

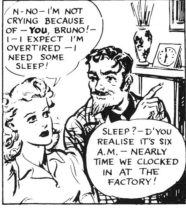

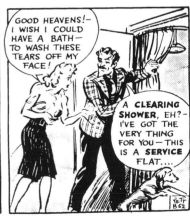

116

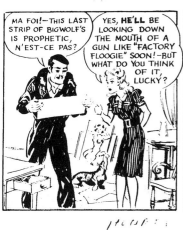

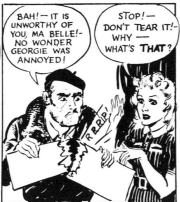

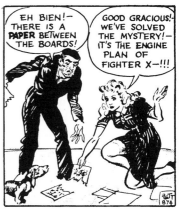

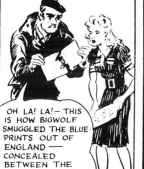

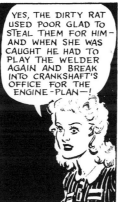

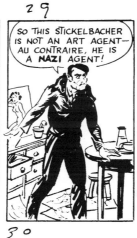

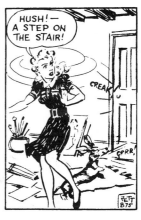

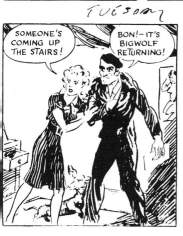

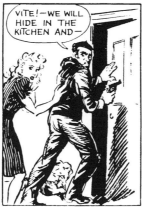

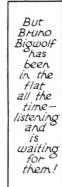

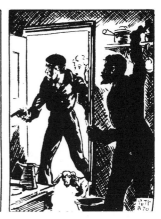

Chapter Eight

Jane – USA Style

With the friendly invasion of Britain during 1942 by hundreds of thousands of GIs and other "Yanks", Jane had potentially a whole new audience. Certainly, most of the American servicemen posted to Britain were enamoured of the girls they found here and a fair-skinned, blonde-haired and lithe-limbed beauty like Jane ought to be a winner. She was, after all, the very epitome of what a classic English Rose should be and with their penchant for our girls Pett was convinced her popularity with the Yanks would outstrip all else. Oddly, the chemistry was just not there and the appeal of our heroine with Uncle Sam's boys could not, in any way, be considered to have been universal or even widespread. Certainly, she had her fans amongst them but interest from the Yanks in English newspapers was limited. For that reason alone, Jane was not widely exposed – if that is not an unfortunate choice of word – to the average GI in Britain. Jane's theatre shows, however, were a different kettle of fish and almost wherever she appeared live on stage a good crowd of wolf-whistling foot-stomping Americans could be assured. Looking back on it in 2000, Chrystabel reflected that although the Yanks loved her shows, she always gained the impression that they had not the faintest idea who she was really supposed to be. She was, though, said one American bomber pilot "… an absolute peach, a total honey". Maybe this was the same bomber pilot of the US 8th Air Force's 446 Bomb Group who named his B-24 Liberator bomber "Jane". With their predilection for seemingly naming just about all of their combat 'planes, and mostly after girls, it could be expected that more than just a few might have carried Jane's name if her popularity had been rather more widespread amongst the Americans.

Despite the coolness towards her by the American troops, the *Daily Mirror* remained convinced that an appreciative and lucrative audience for Jane awaited Stateside. Pushing ahead with their plans to take her to the Americans, the *Daily Mirror* syndicated Jane to Hearst's King Features but found it was not a simple case of just shipping the same cartoons to the USA for straight reproduction. What the newspaper would discover was exactly the same thing that so many other exporters of a whole variety of entertainment forms to the USA have also found out across the years: sometimes, it just doesn't work with an American audience. For one thing, with the Jane cartoons the Americans could just not fathom a lot of the nuances, terminology or even the often less-than-subtle innuendo. And as for Jane's almost permanent state of semi-undress or nudity, that was a major problem. Not even for the American Forces Newspaper *Stars & Stripes* was it totally acceptable, and neither did Jane prove to be anything of the sensation she was with the Brits.

Suddenly, and to keep his masters at Fetter Lane kindly disposed towards the idea of increasing his fee, Pett found himself burning the

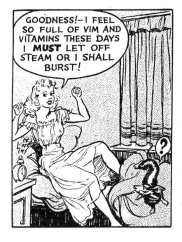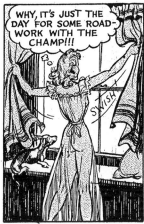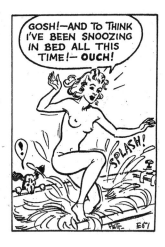

Spot the difference! Jane had to be re-drawn by Norman Pett – censored, in fact – for consumption by an American audience, this being a before and after Americanisation of one particular Jane strip cartoon. Ultimately, the cartoon was less than a success in the USA. This first strip is before the censor was involved ...

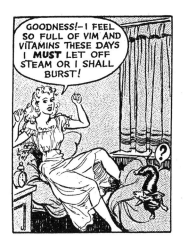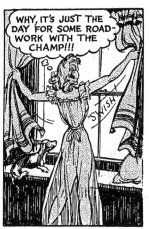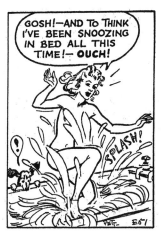

... and this is after.

midnight oil to redraw hundreds and hundreds of Jane frames. In effect, he was instructed to "... make Jane decent". A tall order, but the American publishing regulators would not permit Jane to appear so frequently in her varying states of undress. The solution, quite simply, was to draw in more clothes – tweed jackets over bra and cleavage, slacks drawn in to blank out the stockings and suspenders. Pett didn't like it, and told the *Daily Mirror* so. He insisted that it just didn't work and that the whole point of Jane was being eliminated. The effect, of course, had been to merely sanitise out of the American version the strip cartoons's sauciness, the one remaining element that an American audience might just have understood! In another desperate measure, handsome GIs were more frequently introduced to the strip in a forlorn attempt to widen the appeal. The end result was inevitable. The cartoon bombed in the USA. Even so, attempts continued to try to revive interest in her throughout North America and Canada and shortly after D-Day the American Forces newspaper *Round-Up* made a commentary on Jane's D-Day + 1 total strip. "Well sirs, you can go home now", they said. "Right out of the blue and with no one even threatening her, Jane peeled a week ago. The British 36th Division immediately gained six miles and the British attacked in the Arakan. Maybe we Americans ought to have Jane, too".

Despite this particular journalist's enthusiasm, it still didn't happen for Jane in the USA – although the *Daily Mirror* had one last gasp at taking a slice of the lucrative American cartoon market.

With little notice, photographers and reporters from the American magazine *Life* descended on Pett's Cotswold home to watch and photograph him at work. They did so as he drew a model wearing little else but a suggestion of black lace. The photos they shot and the layout itself looked good. Pett told Fetter Lane he was optimistic that the result would help Jane's American campaign. Then, disaster. In America, the men's magazine *Esquire* was the primary publishing vehicle for the pin-up artwork of Alberto Vargas, and suddenly the American postal services were trying to ban *Esquire* from the US Mail on the basis that the content was too lewd and provocative. By comparison, the Vargas girl was virtually fully clothed even when set against the newly-covered-up version of Jane that Pett had produced for American viewing. *Life* wrote Norman Pett a regretful letter saying they did not consider the time opportune for their proposed article. Jane's American adventure had come to an end, indirectly killed off by her Vargas girl rivals. But what of these Vargas girls? Although not in any sense strip cartoons, they were perhaps Jane's nearest US look-alikes. As such, we should examine briefly the part they played in the history of World War Two particularly as a tenuous link to the Jane story must surely exist.

Alberto Vargas (1896-1982) is regularly hailed as the absolute master of all pin-up artists, and his work has certainly achieved universal recognition and acclaim. However, his art was far removed from that of Norman Pett who, essentially, was a cartoonist and illustrator. For Pett, the fact that his creation of Jane became a pin-up was something of an accolade but for Vargas the appellation "pin-up" was viewed as somewhat demeaning and vulgar. But whatever his artistic pride, and however he liked to describe his work, the fact remained that his paintings became the pin-up of choice for the American forces during World War Two. *Esquire* magazine in the USA signed up Vargas in 1941 and his artwork immediately leapt in popularity. However, *Esquire* decided that their artist's name would sound better if the letter "s" was dropped, and so he became Varga for all of the artwork commissioned by that magazine. As with Pett, Vargas used life models – usually his wife Anna Mae – but sometimes, chaperoned, a beautiful fifteen-year-old red-head called Jeanne Dean. Despite the legal action brought against *Esquire* by the US postal service in 1943 on the grounds of obscenity, it is difficult sixty years later to understand how these tasteful paintings could be so considered. None of his pictures depicted nudes, and the softness of the models' expressions and the non-salacious poses were in a league of their own. Even so, the *New Yorker* reckoned that Vargas could make a girl look nude even if she were rolled up in a rug.

It is not the intention here to draw any real comparison or examine similarities between the work of Pett and Vargas. These were two different art forms and thus no meaningful comparison can be drawn. Indeed, it would be invidious to even attempt to do so. Certainly, Vargas had his admirers and followers amongst the British too, but so did the talented English artist David Wright. His illustrations were much in the Vargas mould, but generally more daring and often nude. Certainly, they were often raunchy as compared to Jane's, or even Vargas', almost inoffensive innocence. Of Vargas and Wright it is true to say that their one-off paintings, whether for gatefold or calendar, were made that both the artistry and female form might be admired. That alone was the sole intention. With Pett's Jane, as in so much else that Jane did, the enjoyment of the art and her form were both almost accidental. As far as preferences went, it was clear where American allegiances lay and one cannot be surprised at that. Inevitably, as with Jane for the Brits, so the Varga girl became the favoured basis for mascots in the American services and there were almost countless examples applied as nose art to USAAF and USN airplanes. That is not to say, of course, that Vargas' art was not also popular with the British. Indeed, Chrystabel herself was always a great lover of his work. As for the Americans though, a limited number of United States Army Air Force and Navy 'planes called Jane are known to have existed, but with almost no photographic evidence available it is difficult to assess how many, if any at all, were based upon the *Daily Mirror* heroine. Some may well have been based on the

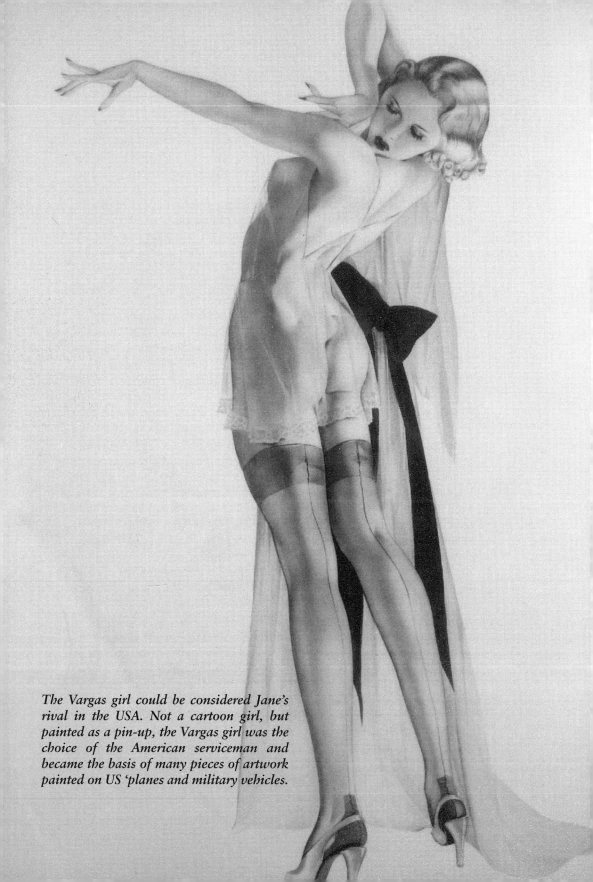

The Vargas girl could be considered Jane's rival in the USA. Not a cartoon girl, but painted as a pin-up, the Vargas girl was the choice of the American serviceman and became the basis of many pieces of artwork painted on US 'planes and military vehicles.

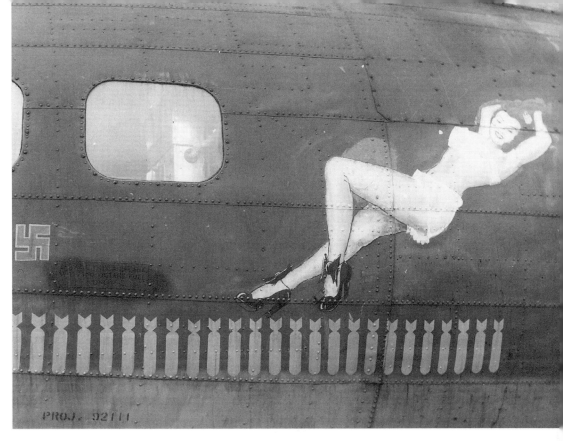

This example, rather crudely executed, used the Vargas girl image as its basis. This girl was painted on a USAAF 8th Air Force B-17 Flying Fortress named "Virgin on the Verge" belonging to the 388th Bomb Group.

Hollywood star Jane Russell. The one photograph traced (reproduced here) of Jane, the US 8th Air Force B-24 Liberator girl, is not by any certainty representative of our Jane.

This English Rose, with her quintessential and almost quirky Britishness, just didn't translate into American, whatever trick was tried. As Pett later said, "Even marrying her off to Clark Gable wouldn't have worked!"

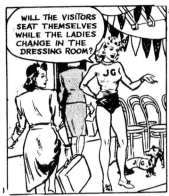

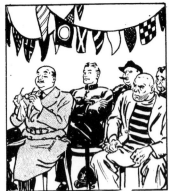

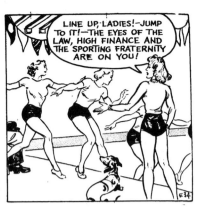

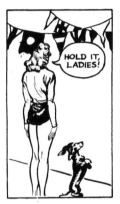

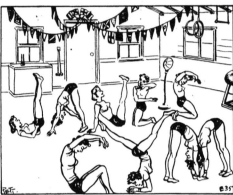

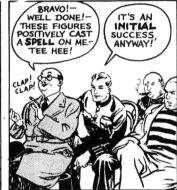

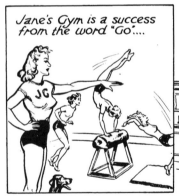

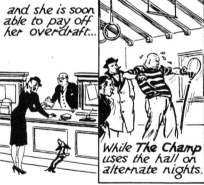

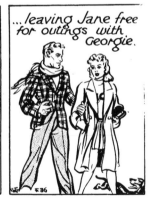

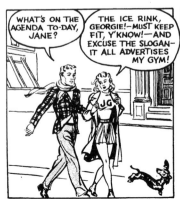

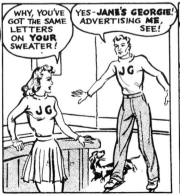

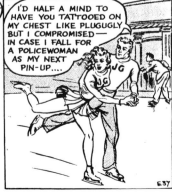

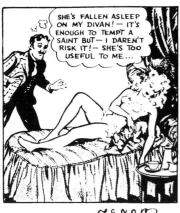

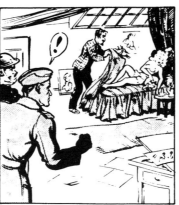

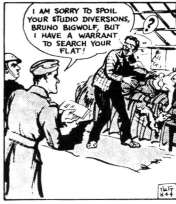

NONOM FEB. 22

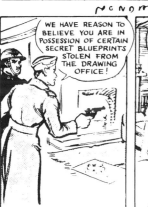

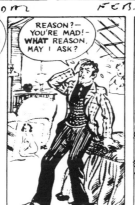

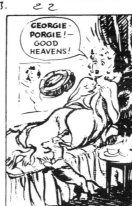

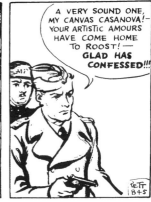

TUESDAY FEB. 23

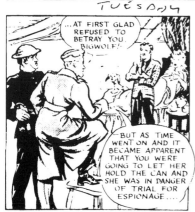

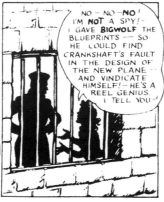

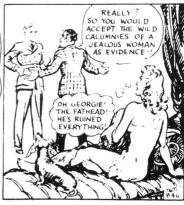

125

Chapter Nine

Into the Sunset

Whilst the fame and popularity of Jane cannot be said to be tied exclusively to the war years, it is a fact that, at the war's end, her following began to wane rapidly. The reasons why are not hard to find. For the troops away from home, Jane had been almost a substitute girlfriend to countless thousands; at the very least, an almost tangible link with that all too rare commodity in any war zone – femininity. Back home, and the soldier had his real girlfriend, fiancée, wife or lover. The need for Jane, if need is the right word, had receded. Besides, not all of the womenfolk back home might be too receptive of another woman, even a fantasy cartoon figure. Certainly, Jane as a pin-up was a non-starter except, perhaps, in the workplace. It is true, as well, that back home there was a tendency by many ex-servicemen to reject things that might be a reminder of the past. All of these factors added to the decline in Jane's popularity as a cartoon, but most of all it must have been the dispersing of the collective readership: whole regiments, squadrons or ships had once followed her exploits avidly and to a man. That was now gone. For the fresh intakes of National Servicemen, the same appeal for Jane did not seem to exist, and in the following few years it was clear that the writing was on the wall for Pett's creation. Decline had set in, and after 1945 the strip cartoon no longer had the immense selling power for the *Daily Mirror* that it had previously held. But Jane the comic strip was to have one last and unexpected gasp in the very immediate post-war period of 1945. Incredibly, it was to influence the shaping of post-war Britain.

Shortly after the end of hostilities in Europe, the Socialists indicated that they no longer wished to continue in the wartime coalition government, thus forcing a General Election. Prime Minister Winston Churchill reluctantly tendered his resignation, and that of the coalition cabinet, on 23 May 1945, but was immediately invited by HM The King to form a temporary caretaker government. Ultimately though, the election was held during July 1945, and with the result that Winston Churchill's Government had been heavily defeated, with massive gains to the Labour Party.

Throughout the war, and indeed through the election campaign, a huge majority of ordinary troops had been loyal readers of the *Daily Mirror* above any other paper. As we have seen, this was very largely attributable to Jane. With the *Daily Mirror* an overtly left-wing Labour newspaper, it was thus inevitable that the same readership would become susceptible to Labour's message. Its following was mainly working class, and comprised largely of young servicemen who had never voted before – all of them looking for that promise of a better post-war Britain, perhaps, even that "Land fit for Heroes" promised after World War One. Labour promised such a rosy future, and the *Daily Mirror* championed the cause. That the *Daily Mirror* as a newspaper directly influenced the outcome of the first post-war General Election cannot be denied. By inference, therefore, it must certainly be the case that Jane had helped, if only indirectly, to play a part in that election outcome. Not only could it be said that she had helped to win the war, but she had also helped to win (or lose!) the General Election. Winston Churchill's mild amusement with Jane now turned to angry frustration, and he is reported to have wildly flung the *Daily Mirror* across his study at 10 Downing Street the morning after his defeat. Eager to soothe, his wife Clementine suggested the defeat might be a blessing in disguise. *"If it is a blessing, then it certainly is very well disguised indeed"*, grunted the great man. It is said that he wanted to see the back of "... *that wretched girl*", although he would still have another fourteen years to wait. In some measure, at least, Churchill was certainly only too aware of the part Jane had played in his downfall. Ironically, of course, Jane herself was totally apolitical – although it could also be said that her background and standards were possibly more towards the right than the left! Certainly, her frolicsome adventures in scant attire were such that Labour's old guard would probably want to distance themselves from her. But she had served a purpose and served it well.

Governments, though, may come and go. Jane remained Jane and the cartoon strip went on. A slight change in storylines would steer Jane away from the more military wartime themes, but her adventures would always involve some degree or other of undress. For a while, and in the immediate post-war years, Pett continued to draw Jane but eventually, in 1948, he "retired" from the job he had loved. Quite why he retired is shrouded in some mystery. Officially, it was due to ill-health and certainly Pett had not always been a well man. It may, though, have been due to yet another dispute with his masters at Fetter Lane or perhaps the copy deadlines and advance schedules had become just too demanding. Maybe he had simply just become tired of Jane and sought pastures new. Certainly, in 1948, Pett had a new strip cartoon called Susie that he drew for the *Sunday Dispatch*. Maybe he could have thought this to be another new and profitable route, although it is entirely feasible that the overall demands of a daily strip were just too much for him to cope with. One strip per week would certainly be a less demanding routine. Whatever, in her last years, Jane was drawn by Pett's able assistant, Mike Hubbard.

HEY FELLOWS! LOOK WHO'S HERE!!!

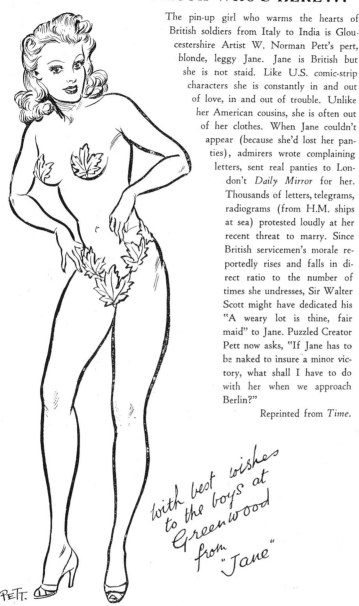

The pin-up girl who warms the hearts of British soldiers from Italy to India is Gloucestershire Artist W. Norman Pett's pert, blonde, leggy Jane. Jane is British but she is not staid. Like U.S. comic-strip characters she is constantly in and out of love, in and out of trouble. Unlike her American cousins, she is often out of her clothes. When Jane couldn't appear (because she'd lost her panties), admirers wrote complaining letters, sent real panties to London's *Daily Mirror* for her. Thousands of letters, telegrams, radiograms (from H.M. ships at sea) protested loudly at her recent threat to marry. Since British servicemen's morale reportedly rises and falls in direct ratio to the number of times she undresses, Sir Walter Scott might have dedicated his "A weary lot is thine, fair maid" to Jane. Puzzled Creator Pett now asks, "If Jane has to be naked to insure a minor victory, what shall I have to do with her when we approach Berlin?"

Reprinted from *Time*.

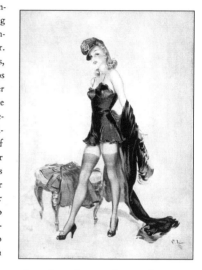

Another forces favourite was the pin-up girl of David Wright, although she was much more of an erotic glamour girl than the naïvely innocent Jane. This picture was called "Off with the old..." and images like this one shared many a billet wall with Jane!

With best wishes to the boys at Greenwood from "Jane"

"MAPLE SUGAR". Drawn by request for OVER SEAS by W. Norman Pett.

Jane's export to North America was not confined to the USA. Norman Pett also drew Jane for the Canadian paper "Over Seas", with this particular drawing of her captioned "Maple Sugar". If anything, she went down rather more successfully with the Canadians than with the Americans.

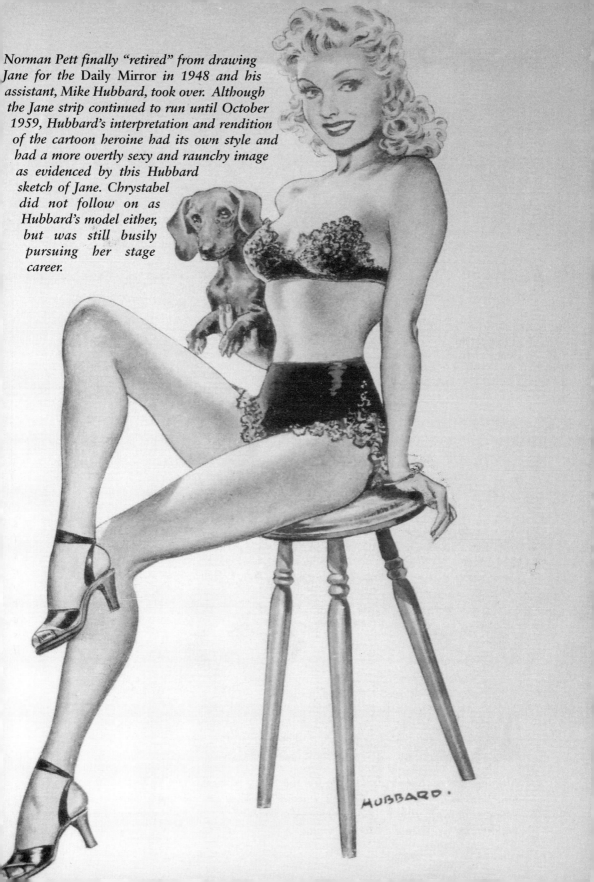

Norman Pett finally "retired" from drawing Jane for the Daily Mirror in 1948 and his assistant, Mike Hubbard, took over. Although the Jane strip continued to run until October 1959, Hubbard's interpretation and rendition of the cartoon heroine had its own style and had a more overtly sexy and raunchy image as evidenced by this Hubbard sketch of Jane. Chrystabel did not follow on as Hubbard's model either, but was still busily pursuing her stage career.

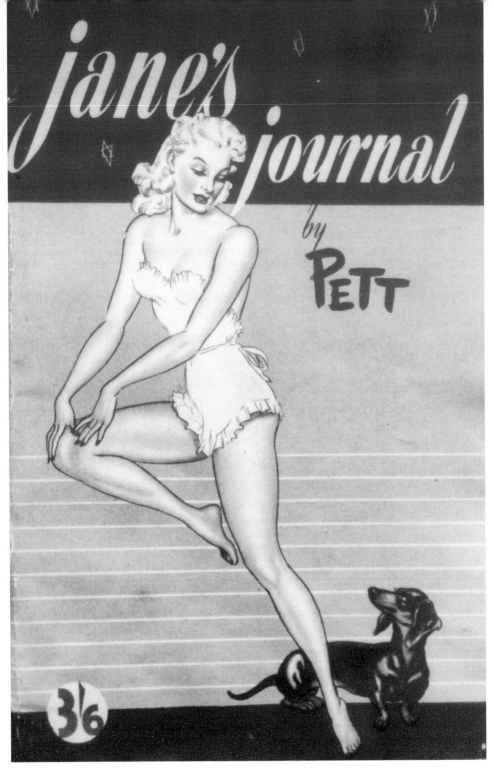

Although he no longer drew Jane for the Daily Mirror, Pett continued to produce Jane material post-1948. "Jane's Journal" was a popular publication amongst devotees of Jane, although it was simply a series of sketches and pin-ups rather than having any structured cartoon format.

Although the line of the stories remained unchanged, it is correct to say that the line of the drawings *did* change. Each artist has his own unique style, and whilst Hubbard emulated his former master to a very large extent, there was a very perceptible difference. Witness, in particular, the drawing of Jane sitting on a stool by Hubbard. Gone was the certain innocent charm of Pett's Jane. Here we had a girl who was far from naïvely unaware of her sexuality. Just the opposite, in fact. An almost imperceptible tilt of the head, a thrusting bosom and provocative pose gave us a different Jane altogether. True, her adventures may have been much the same – but something had changed. It is difficult to put a finger on exactly what it was, but there seems little doubt that Hubbard's Jane would have been rather less acceptable to the girls left back at home than was Pett's. It would not, however, be fair to suggest that Hubbard's artwork was in any way a contributory factor to the eventual demise of the Jane strip cartoon. It wasn't.

For Chrystabel, the transfer of artistic responsibility from Pett to Hubbard clearly meant a downturn in her sittings. If Hubbard ever drew from life, and there is good reason to believe that he probably didn't, then he certainly did not use Chrystabel for his model. For Pett though, Jane lived on beyond the *Daily Mirror* and there was a steady stream of calendars, promotional belts, ties, cigarette lighters, ashtrays and the like that provided some limited work and income for both Norman and Chrystabel. Jane the strip cartoon, as a concept, remained and remains the copyright property of the *Daily Mirror*, but Jane the pin-up character was Pett's. Indeed, according to Pett's family and Chrystabel herself, the copyright on individual cartoons also rested with Pett and subsequently his estate. It is understood that Pett was paid by the newspaper for "one time use", and that the original artwork was always returned under the contract terms. For Chrystabel however, much of the slack caused by a reduction in artistic sittings was now being taken up by her increasing theatrical work – although she also found time for at least one other notable nude sitting.

Sir William Russell Flint was possibly the most prolific and the most famous of all twentieth century artists specialising in the female nude, so it is perhaps fitting that he should have painted arguably the most famous nude of the twentieth century: Jane! At some time during the very early nineteen fifties, possibly 1951, Chrystabel posed for Flint at his Knightsbridge studios, although it proved impossible during the research for this book to identify from amongst Flint's vast range of creations any particular piece that can be tied definitively to Jane or Chrystabel. Indeed, it is quite unlikely that Flint would have identified any of his work thus. However, in 1951 Flint produced a series of drawings called "Models of Propriety" in which he had gently poked fun at his artist's models. Although unnamed, one of the drawings bears a striking resemblance to Jane and, indeed, the pose that has been struck

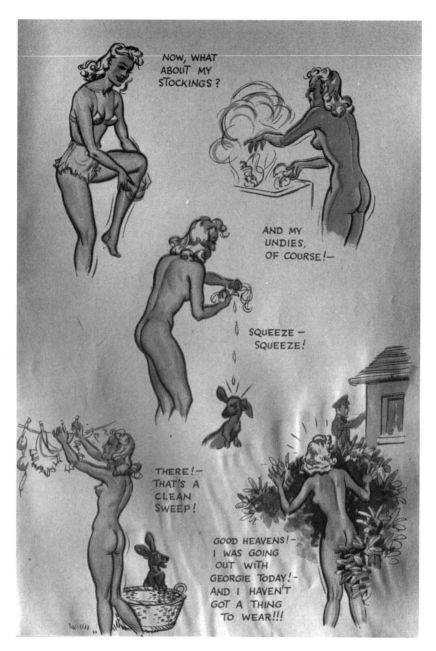

This is a typical Norman Pett page layout for Jane's Journal, produced just post war. These were the copyright of Pett and had no connection whatsoever with the Daily Mirror – the booklets being produced by Rylee Ltd of Birmingham during the late nineteen forties and early fifties. The booklets sold at the princely sum of 3/-6d. There were also calendars and greetings cards in the Jane range, and Pett also drew for another story-book series by Rylee called Angela Darling with words by Gordon Grinstead.

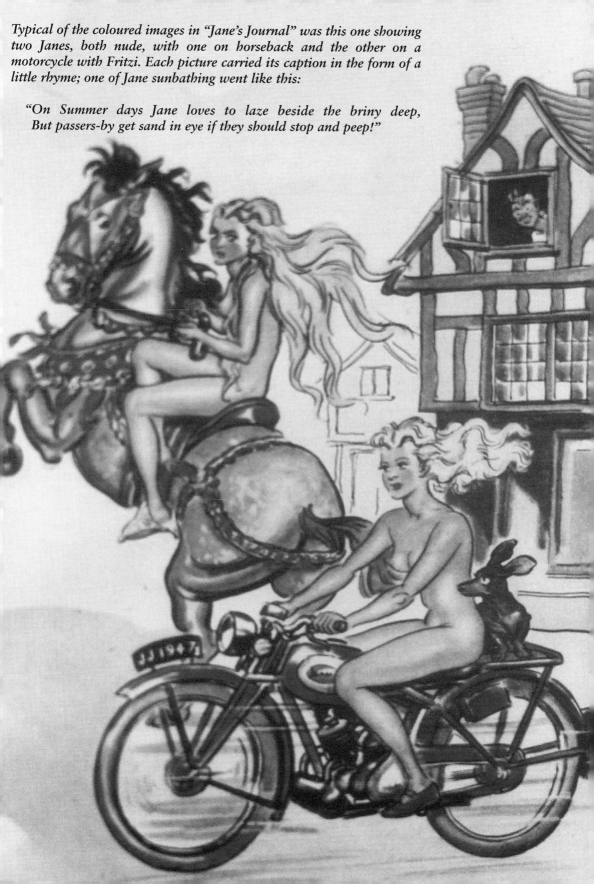

Typical of the coloured images in "Jane's Journal" was this one showing two Janes, both nude, with one on horseback and the other on a motorcycle with Fritzi. Each picture carried its caption in the form of a little rhyme; one of Jane sunbathing went like this:

*"On Summer days Jane loves to laze beside the briny deep,
But passers-by get sand in eye if they should stop and peep!"*

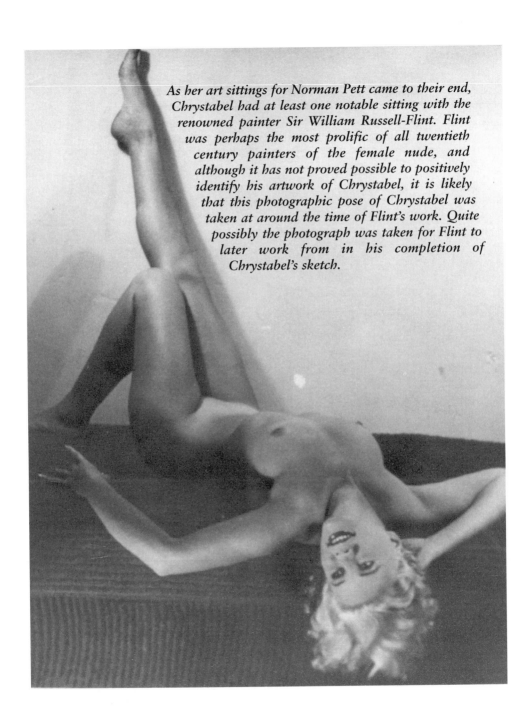

As her art sittings for Norman Pett came to their end, Chrystabel had at least one notable sitting with the renowned painter Sir William Russell-Flint. Flint was perhaps the most prolific of all twentieth century painters of the female nude, and although it has not proved possible to positively identify his artwork of Chrystabel, it is likely that this photographic pose of Chrystabel was taken at around the time of Flint's work. Quite possibly the photograph was taken for Flint to later work from in his completion of Chrystabel's sketch.

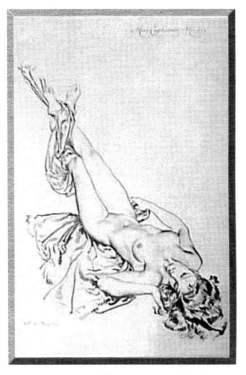

Could this be Russell-Flint's rendition of Chrystabel Leighton-Porter? It was part of his "Models of Propriety" collection, and bears a striking resemblance to the pose struck by Chrystabel in the photograph opposite.

is remarkably similar to one of the nude Jane studies taken by Bertram Park. The story of Chrystabel's sitting remains vague, but there is a sequel to the tale. Some months after posing for Flint, Chrystabel found herself walking down London's Bond Street where she spotted a crowd outside an art gallery eagerly looking at a new window display that was just being set up. Clearly, it was causing quite a stir. Crossing the road to have a look, Chrystabel was confronted with nude drawings of herself. *"I had to pull up my coat collar and hurry away looking down at the pavement in case anyone recognised me"*, she would later recall. *"Despite all of my nude modelling, and the stage shows, it was the one and only time I felt embarrassed and ill at ease. Probably because I just hadn't expected it and it was also in a strange environment."* Chrystabel's excursion into the world of Russell-Flint had been brief but exciting, although she appears to have guarded the secret of it from Norman Pett. *"I didn't want him to think me disloyal, or that I was trying to move upwards from his type of art"*, she later confided.

As the Jane stage shows reached their zenith in the mid- to late nineteen fifties, so the popularity of the cartoon strip began to wane. As it did, the stage shows followed a parallel course and it was becoming clearly apparent that Jane had now had her day. Newspapers, by their very nature, are in a highly competitive world and very much led by market forces. Jane was no longer selling the *Daily Mirror,* and despite the meagre number of column inches the strip took up, there was a commercial need to replace it with something that sold the newspaper: either to replace it with paid advertising space, other more popular cartoons or news copy that would provoke some keener interest and sell. At the end of the day, space was money. Ultimately, the decision was taken to pull the plug and the contract with Hubbard was duly terminated. Pett, by now quite ill, made last-ditch efforts to have the decision reversed but it was not to be. In any event, his health precluded

135

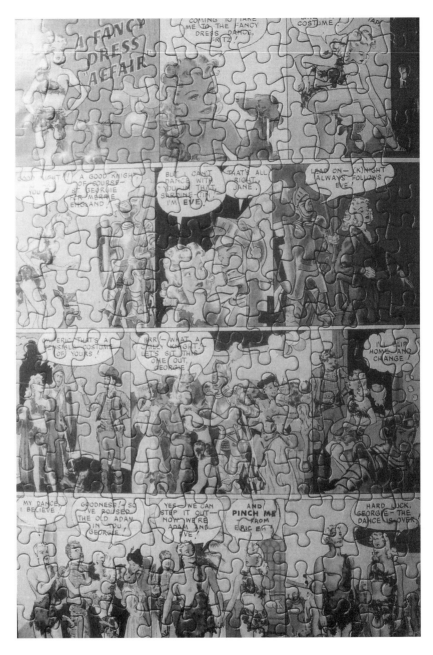

Jane merchandise also became popular during the post-war years. Calendars, ashtrays, belt buckles and cigarette lighters all carried Jane artwork. Shown here is a Jane jigsaw puzzle. Pett seemed to retain the copyright on the Jane brand name, although it would appear that the concept of Jane the strip cartoon remains the copyright of the Daily Mirror, *now* Mirror Group Newspapers.

136

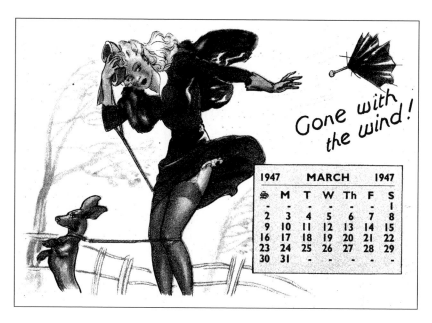

1947			MARCH			1947
S	M	T	W	Th	F	S
-	-	-	-	-	-	1
2	3	4	5	6	7	8
9	10	11	12	13	14	15
16	17	18	19	20	21	22
23	24	25	26	27	28	29
30	31	-	-	-	-	-

More Jane merchandising, this time a calendar page from March 1947 showing Jane in classic cheeky pose and inevitably battling with the elements as well as inanimate and animate objects – all conspiring together against her modesty.

any future involvement with the production of the strip but his appeals that Jane should not be simply dropped, or even worse killed off, were heeded when he asked that a sympathetic storyline be written for the end. The *Daily Mirror*, he reasoned, at least owed Jane, the readers and himself that much. They agreed. The question was, however, how to end that final storyline? In time honoured fashion it was decided that Jane would literally sail off into the sunset with her sweetheart Georgie Porgie. On 10 October 1959, Jane did just that. It really was the end, but such was Jane's fame and popularity that her demise was deemed important enough to be announced on the BBC's Home Service News at six o'clock that evening. Thousands were literally left bereft, incredible though that may seem, and felt as if they had lost a good friend. Once again, protest mail by the sack-load flooded into the *Daily Mirror* offices. But it was all to no avail. Jane was gone for good, but certainly not forgotten. And Chrystabel? She was not gone, and *certainly* not forgotten!

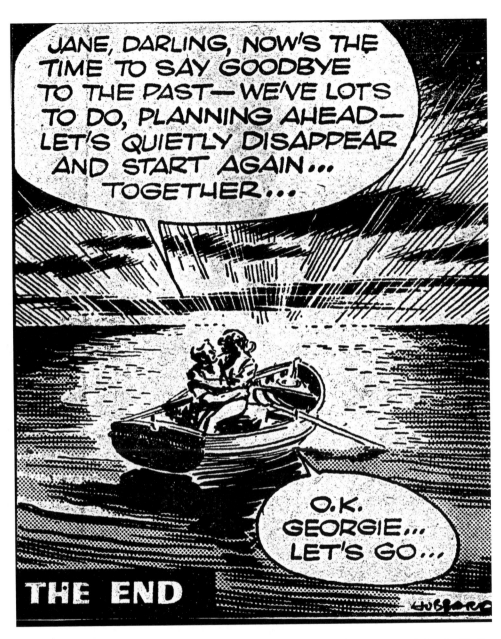

The last farewell. This was the final Jane strip cartoon that appeared in the Daily Mirror of 10 October 1959. In time-honoured fashion, Jane literally sails off into the sunset with boyfriend Georgie-Porgie. In 1934, Jane had been 26, an age at which she was still stuck in 1959! Like her alter ego, Chrystabel was ageless and remained forever guarded about her years – a secret that only emerged after her death.

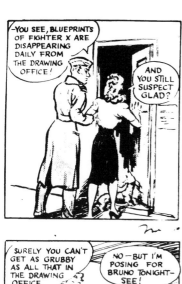

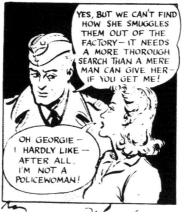

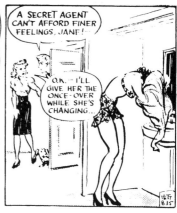

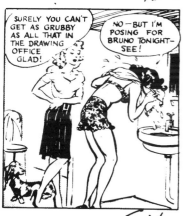

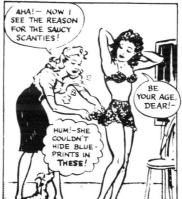

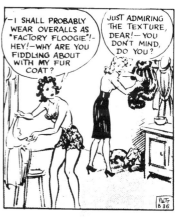

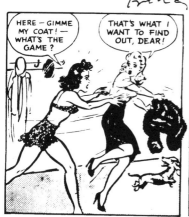

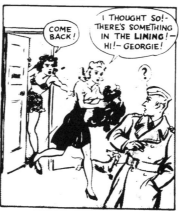

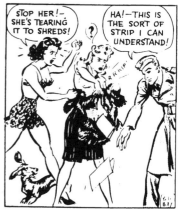

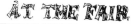

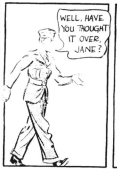

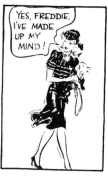

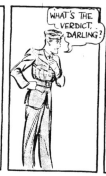

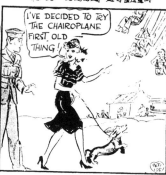

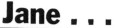

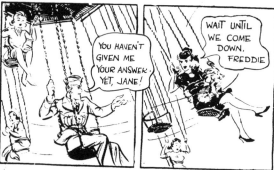

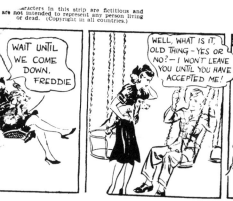

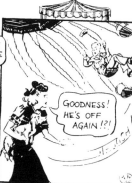

140

Chapter Ten

Just Jane – Always Jane

From stage to silver screen. Such is the path of many an actor or actress who has at some time trod the boards – and Jane was no exception. In the case of Chrystabel's Jane her excursion into the world of film was brief and inglorious. As with all her work – including the modelling for the cartoon itself – no official link with Jane of the *Daily Mirror* ever existed. Certainly, the newspaper never endorsed any such link although it seems to have "used" her photographic image for promotional purposes at periods throughout the war. As for the film, the *Mirror* may well have been pleased that it had distanced itself from it. Indeed, searches of period copies of the *Daily Mirror* reveal not a single mention of Jane's celluloid adventure and not a hint of a review could be found anywhere. Doubtless one review must exist in some newspaper or journal somewhere, but perhaps fate was kind to Jane in not letting us find a single one for the purposes of this book. Chrystabel would have agreed. *"It really was simply awful"*, she later admitted. *"I was no film actress, and the feeble plot and script didn't help much, either!"*

The year was 1952 when Eros Films signed Chrystabel to make the unimaginatively titled "The Adventures of Jane", produced by Edward G. Whiting. An Eros Films publicity leaflet set out the less than thrilling plot:

> *"Jane has a visit from an admirer, an old gentleman who insists on giving her an imitation diamond bracelet. Tom Hawke is in love with Jane, who one day is tricked into going sailing with a "Captain" Cleaver. They have "engine trouble" and are picked up by a Channel steamer, when Cleaver and his accomplice switch the stone in Jane's bracelet with a famous diamond in order to smuggle it into the country. Back at the hotel, Jane, in a moment of compassion, gives the bracelet to Ruby, Cleaver's girlfriend.*
>
> *Next day, Jane is kidnapped by Cleaver's gang and imprisoned in a lonely house from where she sends her dog Fritz to get help. In the meantime, the real gangleader forcibly takes the bracelet from Ruby when he visits the Cleavers' flat. The Police are closing in on the lonely house and the gang bundle Jane into a car and make their getaway. An exciting chase follows and the crooks, after a car smash, are captured and taken to the local Police station."*

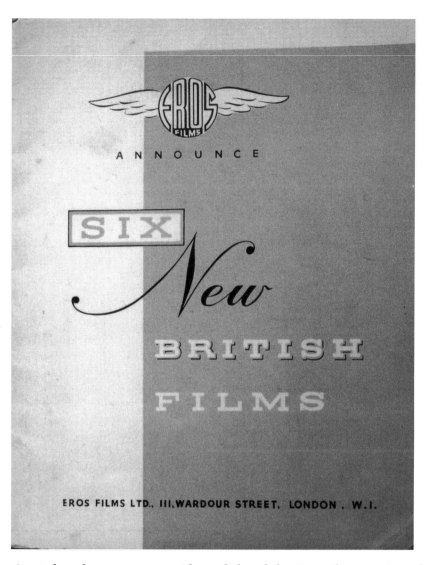

Apart from her stage career, Chrystabel took her Jane character into the world of film and in 1952 appeared in "The Adventures of Jane". This was the publicity brochure from Eros Films who promoted the picture.

It sounds every bit as dire as it apparently was, and Chrystabel implored us not to view the copy held by the British Film Institute Library during our research. Difficult as it was to comply with her pleas, the temptation was resisted, but husband Arthur added his views, too. *"It really was bloody dreadful. Not so much a B-Movie but somewhere down near the Z's I think"*. He too had a part, though. As an extra he was the car driver for the filmed "thrilling chase", shot around lanes in the Sussex

142

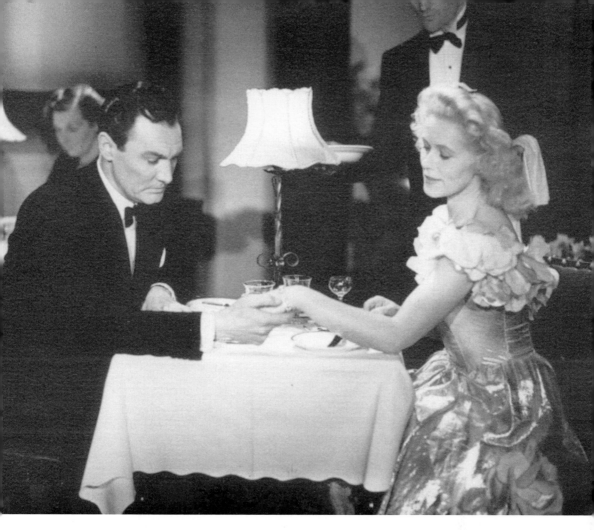

A publicity still from the film shows Jane and the arch-villain, "Captain Cleaver", intent on smuggling a valuable diamond hidden in her imitation diamond bracelet. The film was not exactly a success, and was a low-budget production filmed largely in and around Brighton and employing Chrystabel's husband, Arthur, as one of the extras.

countryside near Brighton and commented: *"There was low budget and low budget, but I think this was even lower budget!"* It was not a particularly auspicious entry into the world of film. But life, and Jane, went on for Chrystabel. Hollywood sadly did not beckon.

With Jane on both stage and in newsprint coming towards its natural end, Chrystabel turned her attentions to more domestic issues and the promise of motherhood. By 1952, Arthur was long out of the RAF and employed as a Civil Engineer, but any family joy was shattered when Chrystabel delivered a stillborn baby boy in 1953. Tragedy followed upon tragedy when their baby girl, named Jane, was born in 1955 and

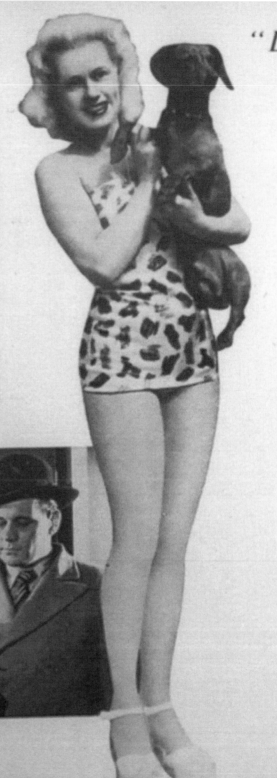

"**JANE**" has a visit from an old gentleman who insists on giving her an imitation diamond bracelet.

Tom Hawke is in love with Jane, who one day is tricked into going sailing with a "Captain" Cleaver. They have "engine trouble" and are picked up by a Channel steamer, when Cleaver and his accomplice switch the large stone in Jane's bracelet with a famous diamond in order to smuggle it into the country.

Back at the hotel Jane, in a moment of compassion, gives the bracelet to Ruby, Cleaver's girl friend.

Next day Jane is kidnapped by Cleaver's gang and imprisoned in a lonely house but sends her dog Fritz for help.

In the meantime—the real gang leader forcibly takes the bracelet from Ruby when he visits Cleaver's flat.

The police are closing on the lonely house and the gang bundle Jane into a car and make their get-away. An exciting chase follows and the crooks, after a car smash, are captured and taken to the local police station.

Mirror" cartoon character known to millions!

"THE ADVENTURES OF

JANE"

Produced by EDWARD G. WHITING

A sparkling comedy - thriller starring "JANE" in person and her dachshund "Fritz"

Who doesn't know "JANE," the cartoon character who became pin-up girl of the forces during the war, and who still charms four million people in the "Daily Mirror" every morning!

Here is JANE'S first appearance on the screen. She's "the real Macoy," too, for the part is taken by CHRYSTABELLE LEIGHTON-PORTER, original model of PETT, Jane's artist-creator. Jane's film adventures create laughter and thrills. A picture everyone will want to see.

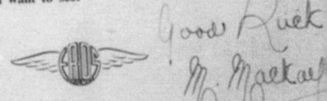

Good Luck
M. Mackay

... and here is more of the same.

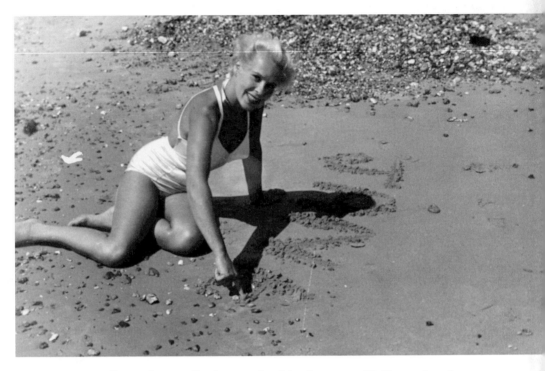

Jane goes to Hollywood ... well, almost! In this glamorous Hollywood-style pose, Chrystabel is photographed on Brighton beach during the filming of "The Adventures of Jane".

lived for just fourteen hours. Finally, in 1957, Jane gave birth to their son, Simon, and the family was complete. In a sense it signalled the end of Jane in her life – or so she thought! Just like her alter-ego, Chrystabel sailed away into the sunset in 1963, heading for a new life in Bermuda with Arthur and young Simon. After three years the family returned to Horsham in West Sussex, and it was here that Chrystabel settled into the role of wife and mother. After the briefest dalliance with variety once again in 1967, Chrystabel became very much Mrs Leighton-Porter. That, she thought, was that.

Not long after her final stage show, and long after the expiry of Jane the strip cartoon, Chrystabel dumped much of her Jane memorabilia including her prized original Pett artwork, fan mail, photographs, stage clothes and theatre bills. A box or two, luckily, remained untouched and packed away in the distant recesses of the Leighton-Porters' attic. Latterly, it was to become a Pandora's box of veritable treasures and memories upon which much of this book has been based. For Chrystabel, the memories were fading with the forgotten box of keepsakes. Then, thirteen years later, Jane was very much back in demand.

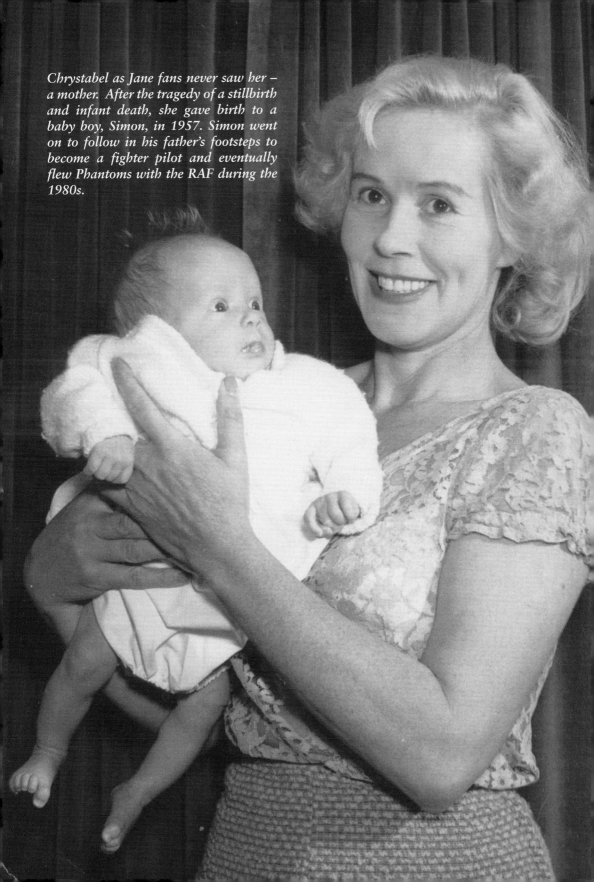

Chrystabel as Jane fans never saw her – a mother. After the tragedy of a stillbirth and infant death, she gave birth to a baby boy, Simon, in 1957. Simon went on to follow in his father's footsteps to become a fighter pilot and eventually flew Phantoms with the RAF during the 1980s.

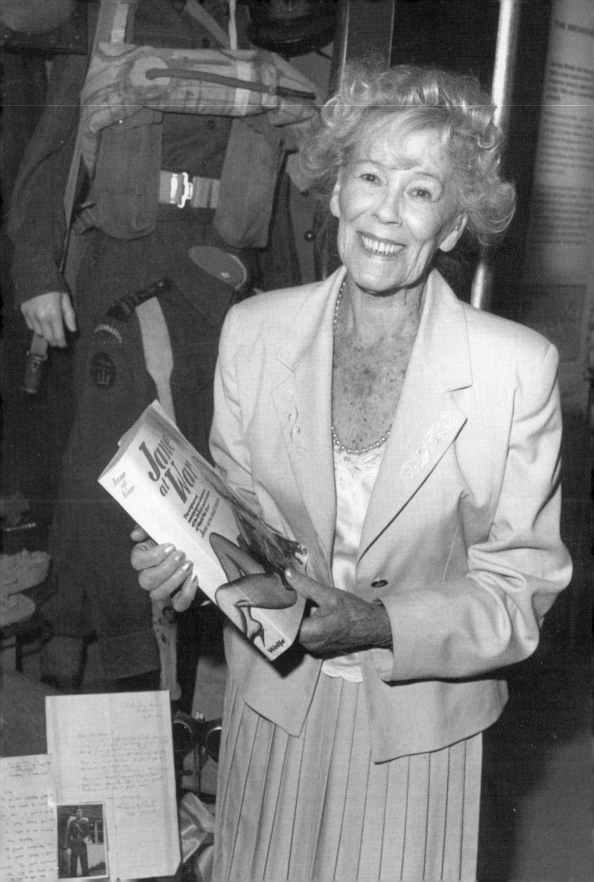

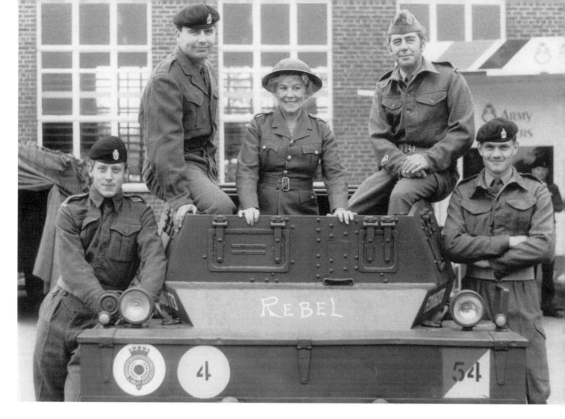

Left: *After the end of Jane the cartoon strip and the last of the live stage shows, Chrystabel was then "rediscovered" in 1980 at the time of the fortieth anniversary of the Battle of Britain. From then on she was in demand to attend events and reunions, open exhibitions, give talks and appear on TV and Radio. Interest in Jane was revived, and for the last twenty years of her life Chrystabel was busy as never before. Here, she is pictured at an Imperial War Museum function to mark the fiftieth anniversary of D-Day and holds a book of reprinted cartoons,* Jane at War.
Above: *To mark the fiftieth anniversary of the outbreak of war in 1939, a local Horsham school mounted an exhibition in October 1989 called* The Day War Broke Out. *Chrystabel, as Jane, happily posed for a publicity photograph clad in appropriate period costume. Had this photo been fifty years earlier then her dress code would have been a little more ... well, interesting!*

"*It was 1980 and the RAF were celebrating the fortieth anniversary of the Battle of Britain*", recalled Chrystabel.

"*Suddenly, out of the blue, I was in demand again. Someone, somewhere had remembered me and tracked me down. Was I really Jane? Would I do some interviews? Did I have any souvenirs of those times? I was completely astonished that anyone was still interested in me, or in Jane. But they were. The next thing was that I was asked to attend a reunion of some Battle of Britain fighter pilot boys down at RAF Tangmere. At first, I politely declined. I told them that I was hardly a girl anymore. But then someone pointed out that they were hardly boys, either. To them I was still Jane, and so I could hardly refuse – could I? I had a wonderful time listening to their stories about me of all people. Here I was, surrounded by national heroes, and all they wanted to do was to talk about me. Well, from there it just snowballed. I was Jane again, and the requests to attend this reunion or that just kept on coming. I tried to never refuse. Of course, the newspapers got interested as well – especially the* Daily Mirror. *In September of that year, 1980, they ran a double-page spread about me under the headline "Revealed for the very first time – the Jane who helped win the war". Well, I suppose they liked to think they had a scoop and that this really was the first time anyone had known about me, but of course it wasn't at all. It was true, however, that this was the first time nude photos of me had appeared in the Daily Mirror and I remember being a bit worried about that. Here was I, this respectable married lady of a certain age, and all of a sudden I am all over the papers in my birthday suit! Worse, my son was then a twenty-something RAF Pilot Officer flying fast jets and I knew that the paper would be in his mess and I worried about the reaction to it all. I even worried that he'd get chucked out. I needn't have bothered. All his chums were thrilled, and his batman told him how much of an honour it was for him to serve Jane's son! After all that, and as the next few years went along, I found myself in demand for TV and radio and of course there were then the fiftieth anniversaries of D-Day, VE Day and all that sort of thing. I was whisked hither and thither by the BBC and even across to France for commemorations on the fiftieth anniversary of D-Day. They took me to Pegasus Bridge and it was there I met Major Howard who told me that the RAF had dropped bundles of the Daily Mirror next day at Pegasus Bridge where there was a terrific scramble to get hold of them to see what I had been up to. A lot of the Typhoon boys went over there with me as well, and it wasn't until I saw some of the graves of the ones who had been lost that I realised just how lucky I had been that my Arthur had come back."*

Anniversaries, guest appearances, opening exhibitions and attending functions at the Imperial War Museum almost totally filled Chrystabel's life for exactly twenty years from her rediscovery in 1980. Suddenly, amongst the veterans at least, there was a reawakened awareness as to who Jane was and what she had meant to them in some of the darkest days of their young lives. Fittingly, and unknown to Chrystabel, a campaign was quietly started to see that in these anniversary years and beyond she was duly recognised with the award of a national honour. In

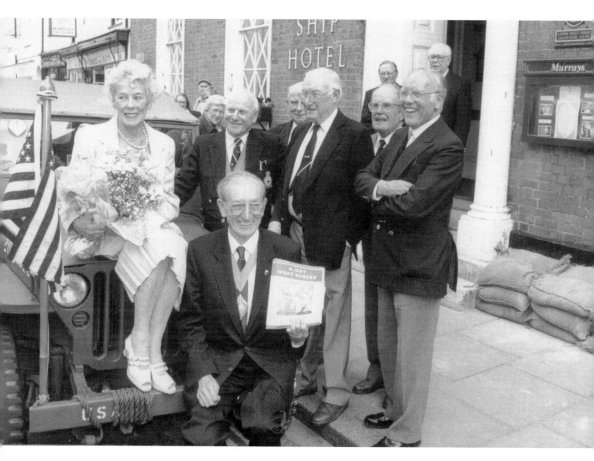

To mark the fiftieth anniversary of D-Day, Chrystabel, as Jane, launched a commemorative book about the part played by West Sussex during the invasion. She is pictured here outside The Ship Hotel in Chichester, atop the bonnet of a Jeep, and with a group of admiring veterans. Standing second from right is her husband Arthur.

1996, and again in 1999, her name was put forward to the Honours Nominations Unit at Downing Street and supported wonderfully by the Mirror Group, The Rt Hon Sir Peter Hordern MP and a whole host of others. Sadly, the 1996 nomination fell by the wayside in just the same way as so many other richly-deserved awards that are never made. Resurrecting the nomination in 1999, Cliff White sought and obtained the support of The Rt Hon Francis Maude MP, although he was told by Downing Street that, ordinarily, to qualify for such an honour the recipient should still be in the same line of occupation warranting that award. Although things had changed, Chrystabel certainly did fall into that category and frequently helped organisations such as the RAFA, the Imperial War Museum and countless other charitable or voluntary bodies. That work, coupled with her wholly immeasurable morale-boosting war effort, must surely have merited some recognition? Sadly, it was not to be. The nomination again fell on stony ground and coincided with the period that Chrystabel fell ill with cancer, an illness that was to ultimately prove to be terminal for her. Honour or not, those who knew and loved her from World War Two through to the end of her life all knew that nobody was ever so richly deserving. She had given tirelessly and selflessly, in her own inimitable way, to her country's armed forces and beleaguered civilian population during their hour of need, cheering and jollying them along. When one considers the honours sometimes dished out to often self-serving businessmen, politicians, rock stars, footballers and the like it is hard to imagine why Chrystabel, the personification of Jane the wartime heroine, should have been excluded. On a lighter note, however, one old soldier later commented, "*Well, we couldn't have given her a gong anyway. Where on earth would we have pinned it?*"

Honour or not, life and Jane went onwards and upwards from 1980. The revival in enthusiasm for Jane even sparked new film interests, both from the BBC and a cinematic production company. With the BBC it was the screening of an innovative living cartoon series of Jane that almost mirrored the earlier stage shows. Starring actress Glynis Barber, the series used live actors against drawn backgrounds and was unique in its format and presentation with the screened series portraying the characters framed by cartoon strip boxes. It went down relatively well with audiences, although it was never repeated – either as a series or in style. Part of its popularity though, was doubtless thanks to its glamorous star Glynis Barber who, like Chrystabel before her, was equally easy on the eye! First screened on BBC 2 Television on Monday 2 August, it had been the brainchild of TV film director Andrew Gosling.

Rummaging in a science fiction bookshop off London's Wardour Street, Gosling came across a book of Jane cartoons that gave him the idea of making a nightly television strip cartoon, using chromakey inlay techniques in which the actors moved against the drawn-in backgrounds. Unknown to Gosling, writer Mervyn Haisman had devised an identical format some two years earlier. Quite by chance the two of them got together and decided to develop the idea jointly, with Mervyn writing the script and Andrew directing. Alongside Glynis Barber, the novelty series included Robin Bailey as the monocled and slightly lecherous Colonel who enlists Jane into some "hush-hush" secret service work. Here, she was pitched against numerous and shapely fifth columnists and the Colonel's termagant wife, an ATS officer. Set in a house called Ghastly Grange, Max Wall played the

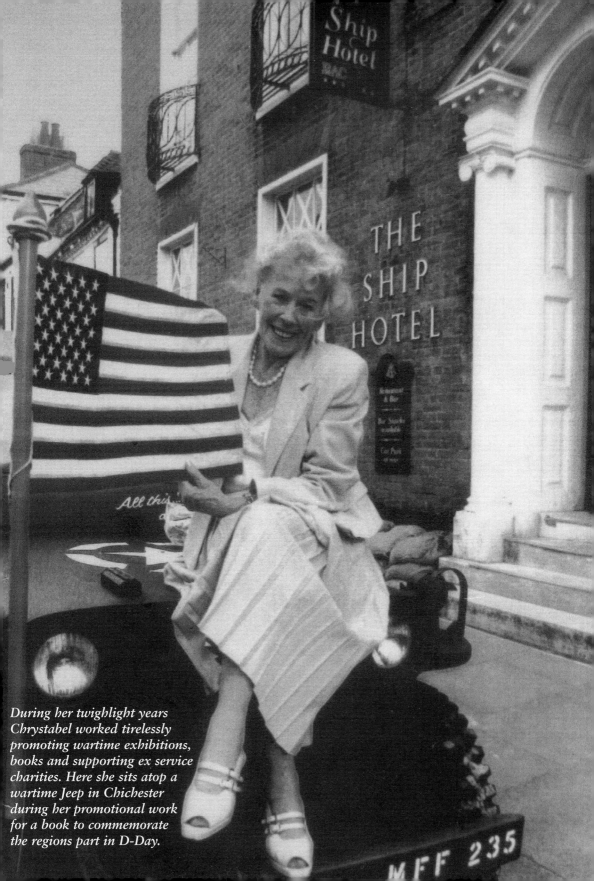

During her twighlight years Chrystabel worked tirelessly promoting wartime exhibitions, books and supporting ex service charities. Here she sits atop a wartime Jeep in Chichester during her promotional work for a book to commemorate the regions part in D-Day.

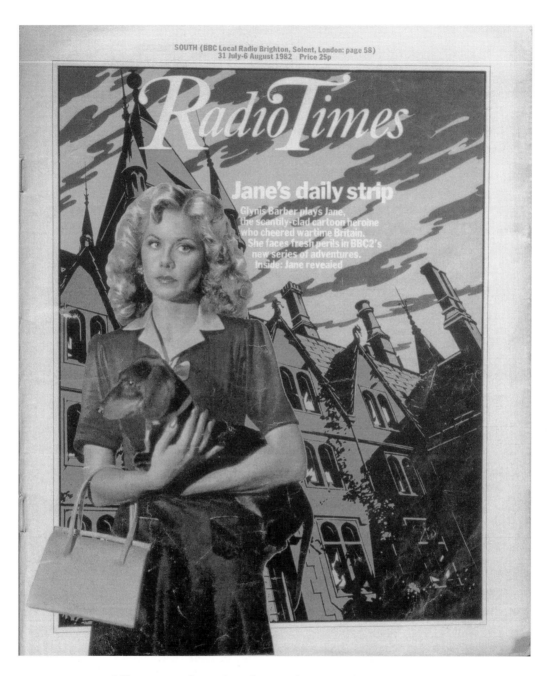

In 1982, following in the wake of revived Jane enthusiasm, BBC TV screened an innovative series of the Jane cartoons. These were living cartoon tableaux, performed by actors against drawn backgrounds. Starring actress Glynis Barber as Jane, this was the front cover of the Radio Times *that promoted the series.*

154

funereal butler whilst a little Dachshund, complete with drawn-in "thinks" bubbles, played Fritz. Needless to say, ample opportunity was written into the script by Haisman for Jane to be parted from her clothes. On the whole, the series was fun and inoffensive and certainly didn't detract from the fond memories most still had of the original Jane. The same could not be said, unfortunately, for the next screened exploits of Jane.

In *Jane and The Lost City*, Blue Dolphin Films attempted to capitalise on the modest success of Jane on the BBC TV show, with the script written again by Mervyn Haisman, who seemed now to have assumed Don Freeman's mantle. Sadly, it really didn't work at all. Produced by Harry Robertson, the film included a number of "B" list actors and actresses. Amongst them, Kirsten Hughes as Jane, Maud Adams as arch-rival Lola Pogola, and comedian Jasper Carrot as the main villain. Despite the fact that this was never a film that was going anywhere near Cannes, or the Oscars, a premiere was held at the Odeon, Marble Arch, London in the presence of HRH Prince Edward. Guest of honour was Chrystabel Leighton-Porter. Afterwards, she whispered that in actual fact she thought her 1949 film was better. The critics were no less scathing:

> *"There are times when one sees a movie and discovers a wonderful classic. A film that makes you wonder why you hadn't seen it sooner, and one that will change forever your view of the fine arts, bringing a feeling of peace and tranquillity over you and all humanity. Jane and the Lost City is not one of them. For the uninitiated it is a silly bit of fun, not all that funny, and with pretty wooden acting – but perhaps, in fairness, that originated with the comic book idea. It tries hard to be campy, but doesn't really work at all."*

It was indeed a pity that what might be described as Jane's final fling was so badly panned. That said, little or nothing could tarnish the memory that would so fondly be held by all those veterans who survived.

Chrystabel, ever the trouper that she was, continued a hectic schedule of engagements right up through 1999 and into 2000, albeit that she hid from the world that she was, by then, desperately ill. Also hidden was her age, by this time a truly remarkable 87 years. The years had certainly been kind to her, and none who knew her would have guessed, or even got close to guessing, her true age which she described as *"57 plus VAT and a bit."* Mentally as alert as ever, sprightly, fit, and in the fullness of health that was the envy of many middle-aged women, she remained so until a terminal illness took hold. For every one of her 87 years she looked and was glamorous in every sense, both in style and in dress. Until

JANE IN THE MIRROR

This Collector's Edition Phonecard features
"Jane in The Mirror" and commemorates the
50th Anniversary of VE Day.

Jane was the strip cartoon character who appeared
in *"The Daily Mirror"* newspaper throughout the
Second World War, and, who helped to raise the morale
of our fighting troops with her daily adventures.

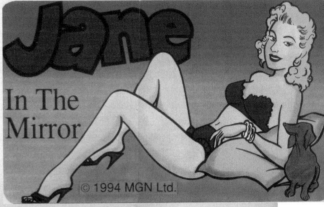

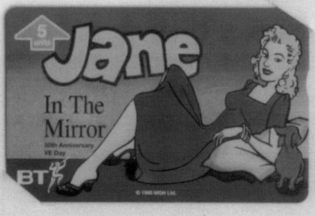

Even British Telecom got in on the Jane act, producing phone cards that featured Jane. This was the original artwork for the cards and had Jane in her bikini along with Fritzi the dog. Interestingly, it was decided by BT that the artwork was inappropriate and in the final version produced on the actual cards a dress had been drawn in. In a strange twist, things had apparently gone full circle since 7 June 1944!

156

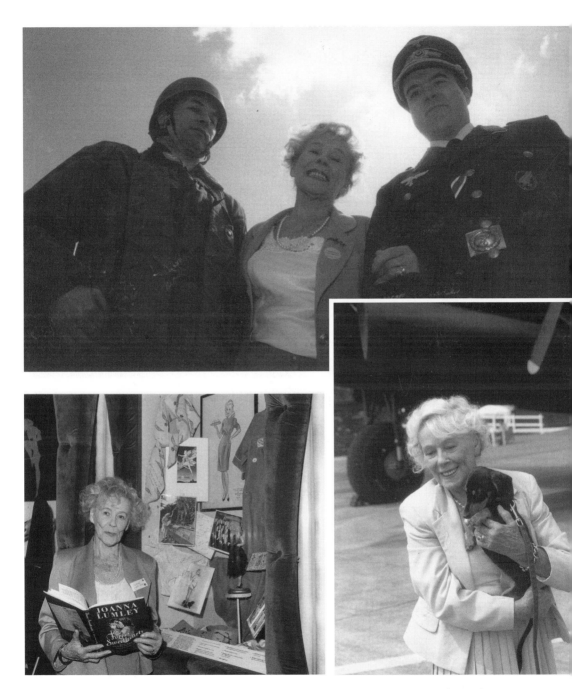

Top: *In 1996 the enemy finally "captured" Jane! Here, two actors dressed as Luftwaffe personnel pose with Chrystabel at an event on the former Battle of Britain airfield at Tangmere in West Sussex.*
Bottom Left: *Chrystabel Leighton-Porter, aka Jane, at the Imperial War Museum launch in 1993 of the book Forces Sweethearts by Joanna Lumley.*
Bottom Right: *Jane and Fritzi reunited. In 1995, Chrystabel visited East Kirkby airfield to view the restored Lancaster "Just Jane" and met little Fritzi as well!*

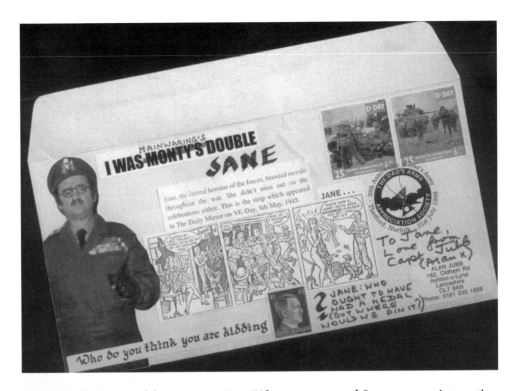

And still the fan mail kept on coming! Fifty years on and Jane gets an interesting letter from an ardent admirer. Could this be the only envelope in history to have passed through the British postal system bearing an unfranked stamp depicting Hitler's head alongside to Royal Mail ones?

the last, the true traditions of Jane were upheld and even when she was very seriously ill she continued to sign books and artwork for charities and enthusiasts from her home. It was in her hometown of Horsham that Chrystabel Leighton-Porter died on 6 December 2000. With her died Jane.

After her death, obituaries appeared in all of the national newspapers including a large column and photograph in *The Times* who, sixty years earlier, would barely have even acknowledged her existence. Naturally, *The Mirror* carried a large obituary under the banner "Goodbye to Jane" that covered almost half a page. Interestingly, however, the *Daily Mail* devoted even more space, giving her a full page tribute under the headline "Jane, our brave boys' sauce of inspiration!" Compare this, if you will, to obituaries afforded other great luminaries and heroes of World War Two and who regularly make only one or two column centimetres of copy, regardless of heroic deeds and derring-do, both in the national heavyweights or tabloid press. Thankfully, the

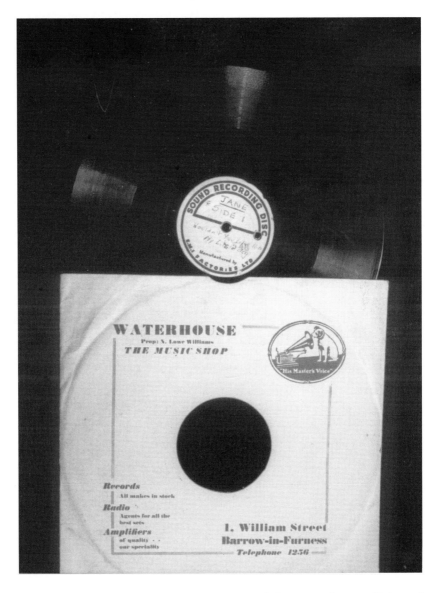

Chrystabel, as Jane, cut a 78-RPM record featuring her rendition of "Wouldn't you like to be my little dog?" Later, she would admit that it was a relief it never went on general release!

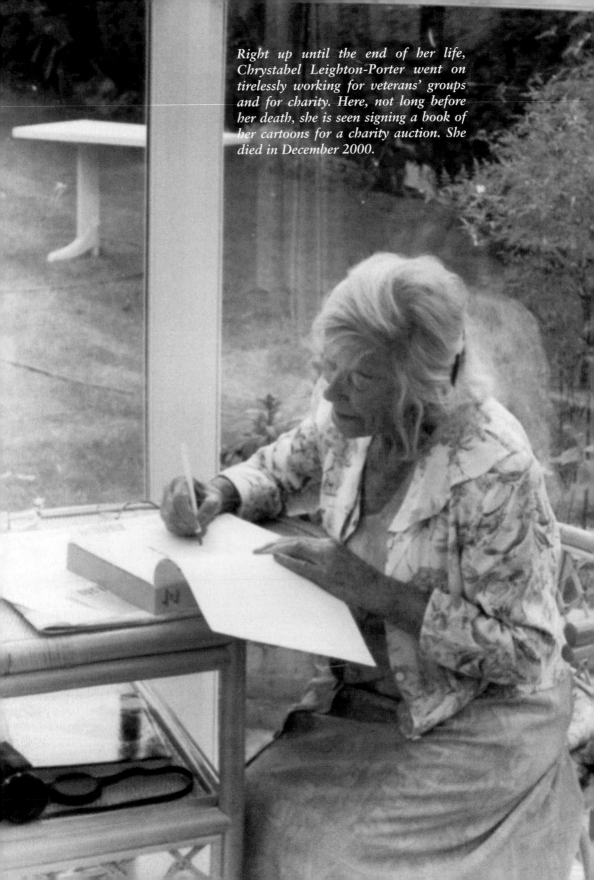

Right up until the end of her life, Chrystabel Leighton-Porter went on tirelessly working for veterans' groups and for charity. Here, not long before her death, she is seen signing a book of her cartoons for a charity auction. She died in December 2000.

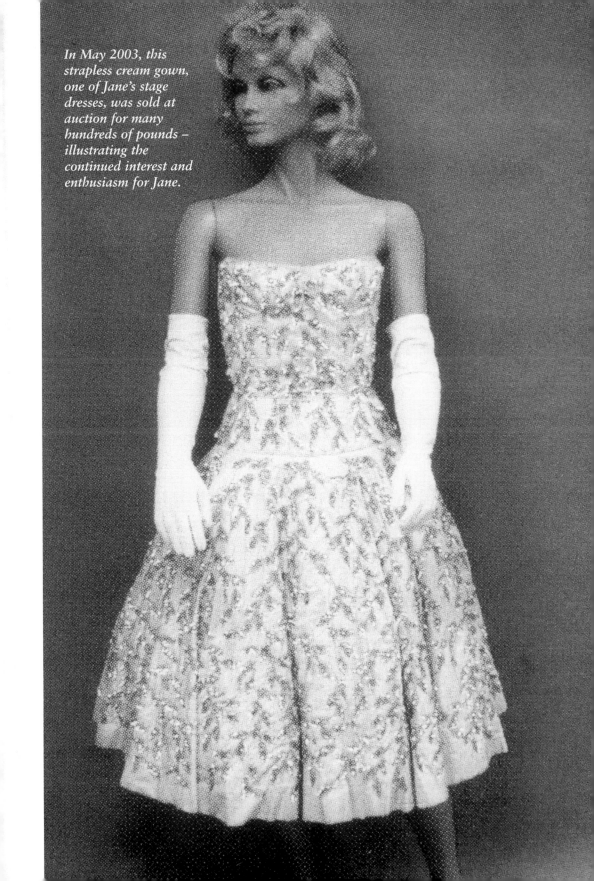

In May 2003, this strapless cream gown, one of Jane's stage dresses, was sold at auction for many hundreds of pounds – illustrating the continued interest and enthusiasm for Jane.

press recognised the importance of her wartime role and honoured it fittingly.

Chrystabel Leighton-Porter, who became Jane and was known as Jane to all, had surely earned the accolade of "Britain's secret weapon". Quite simply, she was just Jane and will always be Jane.

William Norman Pett

Creator of Jane, 1891–1960

Norman Pett was born in Birmingham on 12th April 1891, the son of John Ernest Pett, a jeweller. Invalided out of the Army during the First World War, he went on to study at the Press Art School run by Percy Bradshaw and later taught art at Moseley Road Junior Art School in Birmingham. Here, one of his pupils was Peter Maddocks, later to

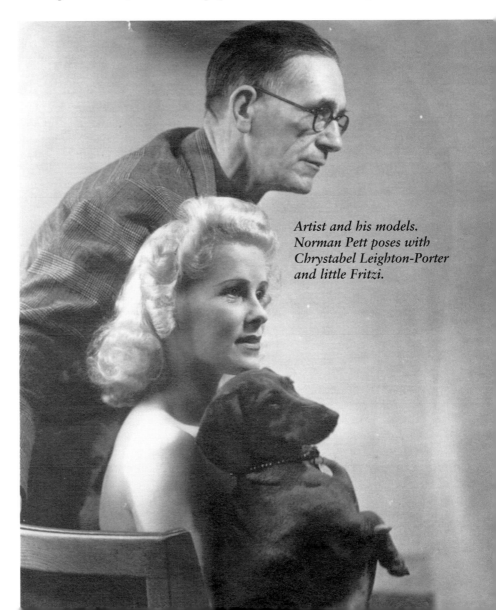

Artist and his models. Norman Pett poses with Chrystabel Leighton-Porter and little Fritzi.

become a famous cartoon and caricature artist. Norman Pett also taught at the Birmingham Central School of Art. He developed his exceptional talent as a joke- and strip cartoonist and contributed work to *Punch*, *Passing Show* and other magazines but with occasional specific commissions for national and provincial newspapers. His strip cartoons also appeared in various children's comics such as *Comet, Knockout* and *Girl*. From December 1932 until he "retired" in May 1948, Pett drew the cartoon strips for Jane in the *Daily Mirror*, his most famous and enduring creation. For the British Army Engineers' training journal *Bulldozer* he also produced Jane drawings during the period 1939 to 1945. From 1st May 1948, the Jane drawings were executed by Pett's assistant, Mike Hubbard. After Jane, Pett went on to create a new cartoon character, Susie, for the *Sunday Dispatch*, where the heroine had the necessary canine accessory: a little white poodle to replace Fritz. Susie, however, did not have the same mass appeal as Jane and quickly foundered. During the last years of his life he produced a number of picture-strip romances published by Fleetway Publications. Pett was an accomplished draughtsman who preferred to draw from life and worked in pen, ink and watercolour. During his career he lived and worked, variously, in Birmingham, Toddington (Glos.), and at Crawley and Robertsbridge in Sussex. He died at his home, Oldland Cottage, Hassocks in Sussex, on 16 February 1960. His work was remembered by millions, and his creation Jane became one of the most memorable and enduring icons of World War Two.